it's all about the
Journey

it's all about the Journey

An effective guide to point you
toward your divine destination

RON J. HAMMOND, PH.D.

spring creek
BOOK COMPANY
Provo, Utah

ISBN 13: 978-1-932898-52-1
ISBN 10: 1-932898-52-2
e. 1

Published by:
Spring Creek Book Company
P.O. Box 50355
Provo, Utah 84605-0355

www.springcreekbooks.com

Cover design © Spring Creek Book Company
Cover design by Nicole Cunningham

Printed in the United States of America
10 9 8 7 6 5 4 3 2 1
Printed on acid-free paper

Library of Congress Cataloging-in-Publication Data

 Hammond, Ron J.
  It's all about the journey / Ron J. Hammond.
    p. cm.
  ISBN-13: 978-1-932898-52-1 (pbk. : alk. paper)
  ISBN-10: 1-932898-52-2 (pbk. : alk. paper)
  1. Religious life. 2. Church of Jesus Christ of Latter-day Saints--Doctrines. I.
Title.

BX8643.S55H36 2006
248.8'4--dc22
                    2005033988

ACKNOWLEDGMENTS

It has been my gift from the Lord to have great friends throughout my life. Ingrid Perkins (she's been the source of more than one book for me), Rheta McCammon, DJ Johnson, Pam Peck, Marsha Miskin, Kaylyn Lorhke, Juanita Smith, Tanya Robertson, Kerri Mortensen, Carol Nielsen, Carolyn Shepard, Dean and Angie Johnson, Deborah Horlacher, Judy Lassiter, Dixie Fawson, Roe Wilde, Alan Wagoner, Kathy Harmon, Koh Kyung-Ran, Drew Hammond, Laura Clay, Marsha Pederson, Gary Hammond, JoAnn Harris, Darla Carlson, Amy Gillespie, Rebecca McClellan, Stacy Taufer, and many others.

Their season of single brought them into our life. It gave me the opportunity of providing strength to them. More importantly, they strengthened me as they endured and excelled in whatsoever state they were in.

TABLE OF CONTENTS

INTRODUCTION

I'd like to ask your permission to teach you. You see, I can't help but teach. It's the one gift I feel I was born with and it's the thing I do best in my life. In my nearly twenty years of teaching college, I have purposefully chosen to focus the materials I teach toward application, utilization, and meaning in the lives of the nearly 10,000 students I have taught. I know better than to assume that I've been there. I haven't. I think I've gained perspective and deep commitment for my friends, family, and fellow saints. How can any of us be happy if another wants and does not have, hurts, and does not heal, needs and is not assisted? So, I ask permission to teach. I am qualified to write a book on gaining strength by coming unto Christ and taking advantage of the blessings He's prepared for me.

You see, I'm on my own journey. This book is a merging of Education Week lectures, singles conference talks, and fireside talks. This book represents an effort to edify my friends, my co-workers, and my family to the love of Christ. As a fellow traveler on your own journey, this book was written for you. Let this scripture from Paul set the theme for its message:

> "For I am persuaded, that neither death, nor life, nor angels, nor principalities, nor powers, nor things present, nor things to come, Nor height, nor depth, nor any other creature, shall be able to separate us from the love of God, which is in Christ Jesus our Lord." (Romans 8: 38-39)

CHAPTER ONE

Your Attitude About the Journey

You are the most important thing to our Heavenly Father. What matters most to Him is the loving relationship between you and Him. The second most important thing is your loving relationship with others. Do you feel your Heavenly Father's unwavering love for you? Do you understand that it's because of His love for you that He allowed you to leave His presence and to live here on earth without a memory of your pre-life relationship with Him; to live in less-than ideal circumstances where you would frequently make mistakes; and to live in natural circumstances that often bring sorrow and suffering? How do you conceptualize your existence on this earth?

Many people live their lives on earth as though they were one of the castaways on the TV show, *Gilligan's Island*. Others choose to live their lives as though they were one of the crew of the Starship Enterprise on the TV show, *Star Trek*. On *Gilligan's Island*, the main characters were trapped. They dreamed, hoped, and worked toward their escape from their current circumstances. They desperately wanted to get back to the utopia of the world they used to live in (which seemed more and more utopian the longer they were stranded on the island). They saw themselves as completely deserted—abandoned, forsaken, and without divine influence. To them life was a state of being displaced, lost from their original homes, isolated from the communities they once lived in, and imprisoned by their accidental isolation from their previous lives. They could hear news from back home on their radio, but never figured out how to send a message to the people back home. None ever prayed. They were "lost" and therefore isolated.

Technically speaking, the *Star Trek* characters were far more geographically isolated than were the characters on *Gilligan's Island*. But, they defined their circumstances in a very different way. They were adventure-minded people who chose the careers that put them in space exploration. They were the futuristic Christopher Columbus-type people who "boldly went where no man has ever gone before." To them life was a journey of never-ending adventures (even though they faced a new crisis and calamity every episode). They willingly went looking for the new places, people, and new experiences that would enhance their knowledge and understanding of their surroundings. They were not helpless lost souls.

On *Gilligan's Island*, the mind set is unhealthy. Even though they've already got it all—a beautiful paradise, water and food, friends, financial freedom, and economic security—they are so malcontented because the island is their only option. They are so eager to have more options that they focus all their energies on obtaining them and they rarely find joy in their present circumstances. They are victims of an accident, not having asked to encounter the storm that crashed their boat on the shores of the deserted island. They didn't deserve the deserted island because they didn't knowingly choose the island. And, as victims, they took control and tried to become "undeserted" no matter the cost to them or to others.

Truth be known, Gilligan and the Skipper chose their

occupations as tour boat guides. The passengers also chose to take a boat tour in the Pacific waters. They are unhappy because the storm changed their plans. You know, I've often wondered which character on *Gilligan's Island* best described me. There's a bit of all the characters in my personality, but I've concluded that I'd be better off trying to be more like Gilligan. His simple nature has a purity to it—lacking the vanity, wealth, snobby, bullyish, unhappy, and intellectually focused personality traits found in his friends' personalities. Gilligan has many traits that represent the healthiest adaptation to his circumstances. He's happy when most others around him are not. He's forgiving (especially of his big buddy who beats him regularly with a hat). He's accepting of himself as he is (also accepting of his friends). And he's very thoughtful to do things for others, even if his efforts sometimes cause more problems.

It's no wonder that most of the group's attempts to get off the island were undermined by Gilligan. What did Gilligan know that the others didn't? Maybe he sensed that much of what they were looking for back home was already there for them on the island. Gilligan seemed to unknowingly sense that even though they were cut off from the rest of the world, they still had it pretty good. A few years after the series was cancelled they mad a TV movie where Gilligan and the others finally got off the island. I didn't like it. Their drama, their united purpose, and their quest had ended. There was no dream world waiting for them back in Hawaii. True, they had more options to choose from. But each was still the same person, just back in civilization again. I wondered if they got back to their lives in Hawaii, if they'd then know how to be content or would they just keep looking for more options. My mother once advised her friend that, "no matter where you run in this great big world to get away from your problems, there you'll be." In other words it's not our location, but it's our attitude that brings about solutions to problems.

On *Star Trek* they found joy in the journey. They are neither lost nor isolated. They had each other and kept regular deep-space communication with the "Federation" (their government). They signed up for their tours of duty, knowing they would rarely be at home, often be in discomfort, and forever face less-than-ideal circumstances. They're far from their original comfort zones and they've learned to find comfort in the new and unknown. They found options within the parameters that their journeys placed upon them.

Which TV show best typifies your attitude about your existence here on earth? Is the main focus of your life to escape your current conditions? (Are you unhappily trapped trying to get out of your current circumstances into "happier" ones?) Or have you realized that you chose to be on an adventure, chose to explore, chose to learn, chose to experience, and chose to see and to do that which you have never done before, no matter how difficult and uncertain the voyage may become?

So, how is your mortal life similar to *Star Trek?* You willingly left your Heavenly Father and Mother to live 50 to 75 years on a distant space outpost called Earth. Simply put, right now you are exactly where Heavenly Father and you agreed you would be—living outside of his presence on earth in your mortal state of probation.

But, you are not on any deserted island. Desertion implies abandonment. You did not desert God and He did not desert you. There's a great plan in motion that governs and directs your life. You voluntarily agreed to that plan and your role in it. Why? Because you wanted to grow and could no longer do so without a mortal body. The body came with an adventurous journey through mortality. Your life is all about a journey (not a desertion) and how you now choose to experience it.

In the scriptures, Adam & Eve, Noah, Moses, Abraham, Joseph of Egypt, Ruth, Mary, the Brother of Jared, Paul, Lehi, and Jesus

Christ all set an example of seeing their life as a journey, a mission here on earth. We see the same in the lives of Joseph Smith, Parley Pratt, John Taylor, and Brigham Young. All of these people were called, drawn out, or extracted in someway from their comfort zones (homelands) to go where they had never before ventured.

How did Lehi and his family handle their fantastic journey from Jerusalem to the promised land? Let's consider the details of their story. They lived in a very prosperous but spiritually difficult set of circumstances in ancient Jerusalem. Lehi was stigmatized because of his preaching and under threat for his life. The Lord warned him that Jerusalem was to be destroyed by enemy armies if the people didn't repent (they didn't). Ultimately, Lehi and his family had to leave their civilized world—a world of comforts, luxuries, wealth, and a familiar way of life.

They walked away into the wilderness, leaving their treasures and home, finding themselves dependent on the Lord for their every need. As they followed the Lord's will He delivered them. The remainder of the stories about Lehi and his children are about his posterity's attitude. For example, Nephi, Sam, and Joseph chose to seek the Lord in their afflictions, but Laman and Lemuel chose to be victims who were "robbed" and separated from the love of the Lord by their own actions.

In the Old Testament, there's Joseph, the chosen son of Jacob. He too had comforts, luxuries, wealth, and a familiar way of life. He, too, had it all taken from him when he was betrayed and rejected by his own flesh and blood brothers who sold him for a few pieces of coin (they sold him only after being persuaded not to kill him by an older brother).

Joseph sought out and found the Lord and the Lord's blessings as he chose to move forward according to the Lord's will for him. Decades after his betrayal, Joseph saved his family and people because his ongoing pattern of Christ-centered choices allowed the Lord to put Joseph in the Egyptian political leadership in such a way that he could bless the Egyptians and his own family.

But, as we learned from the life of King David, if you save your people without enduring to the end (and thus saving yourself) you've foiled the work and the glory of the Lord to *"bring to pass the immortality and eternal life of man." (Moses 1:39)*

Knowing that the Lord's work is to save you, what does He want you to do to help Him with His work? Basically, you have to do your part, even if you're living in less-than-ideal circumstances. Enduring to the end requires that you do your work.

What is your work? *"Behold, this is your work, to keep my commandments, yea, with all your might, mind, and strength." (D&C 11:20)* King David failed to keep the commandments. Joseph kept them throughout his entire life. To choose to keep the Lord's commandments is to allow the Lord to guide, protect, and keep you during your journeys.

Commandments are to your eternal progression as protocols were to space travelers in *Star Trek*. For example, you don't violate the air-seal to the spaceship, lest all the air escape into space and you would be left unprotected from the deadly, harsh, and cold emptiness of space. In short, you'd physically die. You likewise don't violate the covenants you've made at baptism or in the temple, lest your spiritual connection to God would leak out and your spirit would be left to the deadly, harsh, and cold buffetings of the Adversary. In short, you'd spiritually die.

Joseph of Egypt and Lehi kept the Lord's commandments and sought the Lord's direction, thereby saving their families while enduring to the end. Yet, Joseph's life circumstances were much different than Lehi's and most others in the scriptures. You see, Joseph did the solo version of "boldly going." He found himself totally alone as far as family or church companionship was concerned. He had neither siblings, parents, nor extended family to lean on for support. He had no home nor visiting teachers. He also had no priesthood leaders, apostles, nor a prophet.

Discouragement, depression, seduction, isolation, slavery, incarceration, and repeated betrayal were the circumstances that framed his choices. In spite of this, Joseph did what none of the characters of *Gilligan's Island* ever did—he included his Heavenly Father in his isolation. He leaned heavily upon the God of the Old Testament, Jesus Christ. His connection to the Savior came through personal prayers which were consistently answered.

The most important of all scriptural stories are those about Jesus Christ, both in Jerusalem and in the Americas. Jesus' life provides you with two witnesses of how you, as a journeying saint, should live your life. He, like you, chose to leave the presence of our Heavenly Parents. He, like you, was mortal. However, His earthly father was His (and your) Heavenly Father, and thus He was also God. His was the only perfect life, the only perfect example, and the only perfect lesson plan for the rest of us to follow. His was the infinite act of selflessness that saved all of us and made it so that we did not have to experience feelings of having been deserted without divine assistance. Jesus, even though half-God, called upon Heavenly Father throughout His life.

Before this world was created, Jesus began his service. He stood in behalf of Heavenly Father's plan of salvation. He agreed to surrender his innocent life in order to save the rest of us. Most importantly He agreed to do all this while directing all the glory to Heavenly Father (not toward himself as the opposing plan called for).

Jesus taught us about the nature of how He yielded His will to the Father's will. In the Lord's prayer, Jesus prayed, *"Our Father which art in heaven, Hallowed be thy name. Thy kingdom come. Thy will be done in earth, as it is in heaven..."* (See Matthew 6:9-13 for the entire prayer.) In this prayer, Jesus reaffirmed his pre-existent choice to surrender His will to Heavenly Father's. On the following page is a diagram of Jesus yielding His will to His Father's will:

Jesus → Heavenly Father

Jesus not only taught you how to pray, He taught you how to succeed while here on earth by willingly giving your will over to your loving Heavenly Father. Elder Neal A Maxwell often exhorted the saints to understand that our will is the only thing we truly own which our Father in Heaven does not already own.[1] Elder Maxwell also taught that surrendering your will to Heavenly Father's is the only surrender that comes with a complete victory.[2]

Jesus surrendered his will to the Father. Joseph of Egypt, Lehi, Sariah, Nephi, Sam, and Jacob all surrendered their individual wills to Heavenly Father through the mediating help of their Savior, Jesus Christ. Their surrender looked like this:

Joseph of Egypt → Jesus → Heavenly Father

If you follow Christ's example, you also choose to become victorious through surrender. You choose to include the atoning influence of Jesus Christ in your journey here on earth. Your surrender would be shown like this:

You → Jesus → Heavenly Father

King Benjamin gave an excellent talk on surrendering the natural man, which he refers to as being an "enemy to God." King Benjamin taught us to be humble and submissive if we are to overcome the natural man. He gave one of the most powerful sermons ever given in the scriptures about our relationship to the Lord in Mosiah 3:19:

"For the natural man is an enemy to God, and has been from the fall of Adam, and will be, forever and ever..."

So far, this sounds very discouraging. Yet it is true. Since Adam and Eve's fall in the Garden of Eden, they and all their descendants represent a race of mortals who by their very natures are worldly and unfriendly to God. But let's read on:

> *"...unless he yields to the enticings of the Holy Spirit, and putteth off the natural man and becometh a saint through the atonement of Christ the Lord."*

"Yield" has many like-meaning words that you can find in a thesaurus: submit, surrender, give up, and grant. To yield as King Benjamin suggests would be to surrender. While in the Garden of Gethsemane, Jesus bore down under the immeasurable burden of our sins. He asked the Father, *"...Oh my Father, if it be possible, let this cup pass from me: nevertheless not as I will, but as thou wilt."* (Matthew 26:39)

With the weight of countless heartaches, sins, sufferings and pains, Jesus simply yielded. What might we be like if we followed Christ's example? King Benjamin explained that we would:

> *"... becometh as a child, submissive, meek, humble, patient, full of love, willing to submit to all things which the Lord seeth fit to inflict upon him, even as a child doth submit to his father."*

Simply put, you chose to leave your pre-existent heavenly home, but you have the fullness of divine influence for each moment of your life while here on earth. Like Joseph and the others, your best-laid plans sometimes disappear in the wake of others' agency. You find yourself removed from your comforts, luxuries, wealth, and familiar way of life.

For some, where once there was an abundance of comforts, there now lies loneliness and abandon. Where once there were luxuries and wealth, there now lies hardship and burden. Where once there were established goals and familiar daily routines, there now lies disappointment and uncertainty.

If any of these describe you, then remember that the key point is how you choose to experience the journey of your life in the wilderness of your own afflictions. Your choices become the crucial predictors of the eternal and binding end result of your life. Your choices reflect your desires to surrender and ultimately shape the development of your eternal self and where you will eternally dwell in relation to your Heavenly Father's presence.

By definition, you are not a deserter. Deserters have no permission to leave. You and your Heavenly Father both agreed to your life and the terms of it. Also, you are not eternally a "natural" man or woman. You are of divine origin, a celestial being in a telestial experience. Being put in a natural state was part of the terms of your mortal life—to be veiled of any memory of your pre-existent relationship to Jesus and Heavenly Father; to be born with physical and mental flaws; to be raised by imperfect beings under imperfect circumstances; and to be tempted, tried, and proven.

Your eternal self is divine, is valiant, and is by birthright, God-like. Knowing your eternal self is critical to how you seek for and receive divine help in your journeys. You must work at knowing who you really are. You must pray and you must struggle as the prophet Enos struggled in order to rediscover who you really are. (See Enos 1.)

The remainder of this book is designed to utilize key talks, scriptures, and gospel principles in such a way that your journey of discovery remains true and your destination remains victoriously back into the loving arms of your Heavenly Father.

CHAPTER TWO

You Are In The Great Plan

Your soul is eternal. You fit uniquely into the Lord's great Plan of Salvation and your part in this great plan is customized precisely for your individual and eternal progression. Your journey began long before you were born. It began while you lived in the presence of Heavenly Father. There you had friends, you learned, you studied, you loved and were loved. Heavenly Father called a grand council of all His children. You were there.

The great plan of salvation was presented. It called for the creation of a planet. This planet was designed to allow you to live among family and friends the same as you had in the pre-mortal world. Earth would be where you gained a mortal body, were tested and proven, and where you become through your own experiences like your Heavenly Father. The plan guaranteed a stable planet that would host the many spirits who came down to live on it. The plan provided freedom to choose for yourself in all matters. But, the plan gave no absolute guarantees of a safe return for you nor anyone else. God's children could make mistakes in the great plan. But, it also required that one of His children act as a Savior. Jesus Christ volunteered.

Then, one of Heavenly Father's other noble and beloved sons presented an alternative plan. This son wanted to be God, he wanted the glory, and he absolutely guaranteed that you and the others would return so that he could instantly get Heavenly

Father's glory. A war of ideals and values was waged.

You were a defender of the faith. You begged, persuaded, testified, and plead with your friends to be loyal to Heavenly Father and his plan. You and others you persuaded chose the correct plan. One-third of Heavenly Father's other children did not. They were cast down with the Adversary to be damned— never to gain a body, never to progress eternally.

How vast was this war? Demographers who study populations of the world estimate conservatively that 75 billion people have ever lived on the earth. If this number were in fact the case, then those 75 billion people equal 37.5 billion plus 37.5 billion, or one-third plus one-third of Heavenly Father's children from the pre-mortal world. That implies that at least 37.5 billion other spirits chose the wrong plan and lost their right to progress eternally.

Why would your loving Heavenly Father let 37.5 billion of His own children self-destruct this way? Agency. Heavenly Father respects and abides by the law of choice. He wisely knows that righteousness cannot be forced upon an individual. He knows that agency was the foundation for you to become like Him. He allowed those billions of wayward children to suffer the consequences of their choices.

Conversely, He will support any gesture of righteousness, no matter how small, because He is deeply committed to your exaltation. He will protect you, nurture you, heal you and forgive you, but never, ever force you.

The great plan of salvation included three pillars: a creation, a fall of man, and the Atonement by Jesus Christ to save all from mankind's fall. You participated in each of these. First, you helped in the great creation. The earth was pre-designed. (Read Genesis, Moses, and Abraham, which all discuss the creation in various detail). Once a blueprint was finalized, matter was collected from space and organized into the earth. The sun, the moon, and the stars were placed in the heavens to shed their light upon the earth.

Plants and animals were placed upon the earth. Adam and Eve were placed in the Garden of Eden.

So far, most know these doctrinal truths. Yet, far more detail is available in a careful study of the *Pearl of Great Price* and other resources. Consider your own journey while reading these 20 documented truths about yourself and the great plan of salvation:

Before you came to earth:

1. You lived in the presence of your Heavenly Father. He and the Lord lived (lives) on a planet named Kolob—a planet made up of a "globe like a sea of glass." You chose to accept Heavenly Father's plan while one-third of your pre-existent siblings did not. (See Moses 4 and Abraham 3, as well as D&C 130:7.)

2. You are not on a planet that sits untended. Kolob is the governing planet of earth and all planets like it. (Abraham 3:3).

In the Garden of Eden, before the fall of man:

3. During the Garden of Eden era, earth was not in its current place in space. Earth was near Kolob. Adam was governed by Kolob's time until he and Eve partook of the fruit and fell. (See Abraham 5:13 and Brigham Young, *Journal of Discourses*, 17:143-144.)

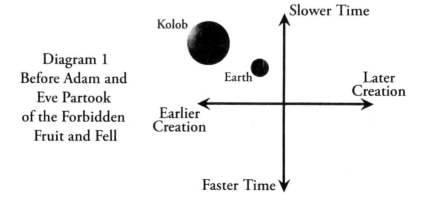

Diagram 1
Before Adam and
Eve Partook
of the Forbidden
Fruit and Fell

Out of the Garden of Eden, after the fall of man:

4. The reckoning of time is different on Kolob than on earth. One thousand years on earth is as one day with the Lord in heaven. (See 2 Peter 3:8 and Abraham 3:4.)

5. God has appointed a variety of times—God's time, angel's time, prophet's time, man's time. And the planet you live on determines which time you are governed by. (See D&C 130:4.)

6. Time is only measured unto man. (See Alma 40:8.) God makes reference to *"time"* so that we can conceptualize how things work on our's and His' world. You were born into earth's time.

7. The earth fell or literally moved through space from the very presence of God (near Kolob) to its current place in "this planetary system." (See Brigham Young, *Journal of Discourses*, 17:143-144.) You were born into the fallen state of mankind.

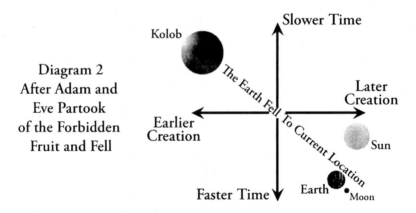

Diagram 2
After Adam and
Eve Partook
of the Forbidden
Fruit and Fell

While you are here on earth:

8. Your time is limited and precious. Now is your time for you to repent, to serve, and to prepare to meet God. (See Alma 34:32; 42:4.)

9. Your life is a probationary state. (See Alma 12:24.)

10. If you are faithful in your time (here on earth) you shall inherit Heavenly Father's kingdom. (See D&C 72:4.)

11. You have a time appointed for you to die. (See D&C 42:43-48.)

After you die:

12. You will perform God's work while in the Spirit World. (See D&C 138:57.)

13. You will be resurrected in a time appointed for you. (See Alma 40:9.)

14. You will be judged and found wanting. But, Jesus Christ's Atonement will make up the difference in your weaknesses and the demands of justice requisite to entering into God's presence. (See D&C 76:59-69.)

15. You and the other faithful saints shall come forth sooner than the unjust. (See D&C 76:64-65 and 76:85.) You're only born veiled once. You will remember all when resurrected and your intelligence will be resurrected with you. (See D&C 130:18.)

Before the Lord's Second Coming:

16. The sun shall be darkened, and the moon shall not give her light, and the "Stars shall fall from heaven and the powers of heaven will be shaken." (See Matthew 24:29.)

17. The earth will be renewed and receive its paradisiacal glory. (See Article of Faith 10.)

18. The earth will return again to the presence of Heavenly Father (near Kolob) and leave its current place in our planetary system. (See Brigham Young, *Journal of Discourses*, 17:143-144.)

19. Christ will return to the earth (in its restored place and renewed state) and after the Millennium the earth will become "sanctified and immortal," made into a planet like unto Kolob—a crystal sphere Urim and Thummim." (See D&C 130:9.)

20. You will live with Christ, on a renewed earth, and nearer Kolob than earth currently is. (See D&C 130:9 and Brigham Young, *Journal of Discourses*, 17:143-144.) You're involved in all of this. You are a full-fledged child of God, a member of His kingdom, and a participant in the great plan of salvation.

So your journey, the earth's journey, and billions and billions of other people's journeys fit neatly into the overriding framework of a master plan that only a perfect being could come up with. It allows for the vast diversity of the agency of all mankind, including yours. Understanding time and how it was created for earth—a thousand years on earth is like a day in heaven—helps you to see the relative insignificance of the length of your mortal life in comparison to your eternal existence. According to Kolob's time you live between 60 and 90 minutes.

But, wow! The importance of what you do with your hour and a half is so crucial! It's like right now you are in a huge airport terminal. You can choose any gate or plane you want for your journey. Ultimately your choices will either lead to a destination within Heavenly Father's presence or beyond it. You must choose well.

The same was true for Adam and Eve, except they began in the Garden of Eden. Once Adam and Eve sinned, Heavenly Father, respected their agency and the consequences of it and cast them from the Garden of Eden. He also cast the earth from its close proximity to Kolob. The earth fell along with Adam and Eve. Now, if you or I sin we can repent. If we sin seriously we can ask our bishop for help with repentance. If we "mega-sin" we may lose our membership in the Church, but we can still go to the Lord through the bishop or stake president to repent and eventually return to full membership.

It's highly improbable that you or I can sin enough to be forever "cast out." But, we can sin enough to be chained by Satan in misery. The key is to recognize when you've made a mistake, feel and recognize Godly sorrow for having jeopardized your relationship with God; confess to God or proper priesthood authority (it isn't enough to confess to a friend or family member if the sin is serious); make restitution where possible; then forsake the sin, never to do it again.

Following these essential steps is so important because you have to truly repent in order to feel clean and whole again. A partial repentance keeps the chains of Satan around your neck until removed properly. After you've partaken of the sacrament again, after having been given the go ahead by the bishop, or by the stake president, you know in the core of your soul that the Atonement is real and that it cleansed you of any chains of evil that could damn your eternal progression. Your journey must include repentance for you to arrive back into your Heavenly Father's presence. Repent sooner than later.

Your journey, now, in this dispensation indicates something very special about your eternal nature. Elder Theodore M. Burton discussed your role on this earth at this time in the history of man. He said:

> "...according to the plan of salvation you were reserved or held back in the heavens as special spirit children to be born in a time and at a place where you could perform a special mission in life...God reserved for these days some of his most valiant sons and daughters. He held back for our day proved and trusted children." [3]

Elder Burton also explained how powerful the adversary would be in the latter days and how Heavenly Father needed his best, his most noble spirits to "limit Satan's destructiveness" before the Lord comes again.

Thus, among the two-thirds valiant in the pre-mortal world, you are also numbered among the most valiant. You represent the final defensive line in the continuing war of ideals and values between good and evil. You must, as you did before, hold that line in all you say and do.

Elder Richard G. Scott talked about how to experience the joy of the plan of salvation and specifically discussed the things we can do to receive the greatest happiness and blessings from this earth experience. He said:

> "Study the scriptures, pondering their content, and praying to understand them. Carefully study and use the proclamation of the First Presidency and the Twelve on the family. It was inspired of the Lord. . . . Listen to the voice of current and past prophets. Their declarations are inspired. You may verify that counsel in your own mind and heart by praying about it as it applies to your special circumstances. . . . Obey the inner feelings that come as promptings from the Holy Ghost. Those feelings are engendered by your righteous thoughts and acts and your determination to seek the will of the Lord and to live it. When needed, seek counsel and guidance from parents and your priesthood leaders."[4]

You live here on earth, isolated in what I like to call a "graduate school of exaltation." Our Heavenly Father is the president of the university, His prophets and apostles, stake presidents and bishops, and other leaders are the professors. You, your friends, and family are, at times student-teachers. You're earning a Ph.D. in becoming like Heavenly Father. (The metaphor continues that you earned your bachelor's degree in the pre-mortal world in preparation for mortality and after you are resurrected you will begin your profession.)

Here, on earth, your agency and how you choose to use it determines to a great extent the quality of your education and the person you become. You have the "now" to prove yourself in order to prepare to meet God, to serve others, and to do good works. But the adversary torments and tortures you because he wants to steal your agency while you are here on the earth. He also wants to make you a "captive spirit" under his tyrannical rule. And he can do it, too, if you let him. Alma taught:

> *"...then cometh a second death, which is a spiritual death; then is a time that whosoever dieth in his sins, as to a temporal death, shall also die a spiritual death...and then is the time that they shall be chained down to an everlasting destruction according to the power and captivity of Satan, he having subjected them according to his will." (Alma 12:16-17)*

Before life on earth ever had a chance to begin, the devil tricked billions into damned states. And he has tricked billions more during their mortal probation. If you are not repentant, he will trick you. Alma warned that the *"adversary snares men...in order to subject them to his will ... to chain you down to an everlasting destruction." (Alma 12:6)* But the Lord, our Savior Jesus Christ, is more powerful and can break any satanic chains that bind us. Alma 13:28-30 teaches:

> *"But that ye would humble yourselves before the Lord, and call on his holy name, and watch and pray continually, that ye may not be tempted above that which ye can bear, and thus be lead by the Holy Spirit, becoming humble, meek, submissive, patient, full of love and all long suffering;*
>
> *"Having faith on the Lord; having a hope that ye shall receive eternal life; having the love of God always in your hearts, that ye may be lifted up at the last day and enter into his rest.*
>
> *"And may the Lord grant unto you repentance, that ye may not bring down his wrath upon you, that ye may not be bound down by the chains of hell, that ye may not suffer the second death."*

Nothing about the battle between good and evil has really changed between the pre-mortal world and earth. The adversary wanted to steal all the glory at the expense of your freedom there, and he will do anything to steal it from you now. Drugs, alcohol, tobacco, pornography, shopping, eating, purchasing, possessing, entertaining, succeeding, and many other activities can be used to snare you during your journey. Addictions are born from the adversarial emotion of shame, and will be discussed later. Addictions steal your agency while binding you with mortal chains too strong for you to escape without the Lord's help.

In order to return to live with your Heavenly Father, you have to do His will now. Because "now" flees with each passing moment you can't afford to procrastinate. As already mentioned, on a pre-specified future day, hour, minute, and second you will die. The Lord has appointed a time for you to leave this earth and journey on to the world of spirits. Before you are judged you will most likely journey through the world of spirits. There, you will be asked to serve and bring others unto Heavenly Father. Every LDS modern-day account of the Spirit World describes it as a place of industry and service for the righteous. (See D&C 138.)

On a pre-specified future moment you will be judged and resurrected. Unfortunately, you will be found less than qualified to enter into Heavenly Father's presence. Fortunately, in the great plan that undergirds this entire process, you have a friend like no other. Jesus Christ, through his infinite grace will step in at your request and endow you with all you stand in need of to make up for all of your deficits. Because of Jesus, you will graduate at the end of your journey, after all you can do.

Elder Bruce R. McConkie described how Jesus and Heavenly Father had visited the Prophet Joseph Smith in the Sacred Grove. He discussed your friendship with Jesus Christ when he said:

> *"He has appeared many other times to converse with his earthly friends; and in the not so distant future he will come again, with ten thousand of his angels, in all the glory of his Father's kingdom, to usher in his personal reign of righteousness*

and peace...He is our friend, our lawgiver, our king, and our Lord. We seek his face and desire to dwell in his presence. We are his people, the sheep of his fold. Our desire is 'to be reconciled to God' through his blood, 'for we know that it is by grace that we are saved, after all we can do.'" [5]

A time for your resurrection will be appointed (depending on how you handle the now) and you will receive a perfected body. You really write your own judgement as far as when you are resurrected and where you will spend eternity. You can't be exalted without Christ.

The place you will live after your resurrection will be on earth. But the earth will be different. Moments before Jesus' second coming, the sun and moon will become darkened and the stars will appear to fall from the heavens while the "powers of heaven" shake. You may see this from the Spirit World or from the mortal world. Either way, the stars won't really fall. They will only appear to fall as the earth is returned to its original location near Kolob. (This should resemble stars and how they streak in space movies when the spaceship travels at light or "warp" speed.)

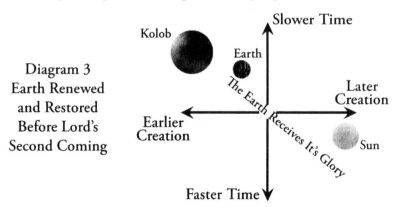

Diagram 3
Earth Renewed
and Restored
Before Lord's
Second Coming

The earth will be renewed and will receive its paradisiacal glory. That means your journey will enter an "easier state." It will no longer be disease-ridden; no longer be catastrophe-ridden; and no longer frail—but, glorified, immortal, sanctified, and like a crystal sphere. Jesus Christ will dwell on earth with you. You will live with your Savior in the physical near-presence of God and in an earthly state that is terrestrial (no longer telestial).

As mentioned, the great plan of salvation is customized personally for you. Look at what Nephi said in the very first verse of the *Book of Mormon*:

> *"I, Nephi, having been born of goodly parents, therefore I was taught somewhat in all the learning of my father; and having seen many afflictions in the course of my days, nevertheless, having been highly favored of the Lord in all my days; yea having had a great knowledge of the goodness and mysteries of God..." (1 Nephi 1:1)*

Nephi states that he had been highly afflicted, yet knew of the goodness of the Lord, having been "highly favored of the Lord." The same holds true for you, your afflictions in your mortal state are the Lord's customized plan for you in your Ph.D. graduate program. They will teach you of the goodness and favor the Lord holds for you.

Just like a physical trainer prepares a professional athlete by assigning specific exercises, stretches, and workouts; your loving Savior prepares afflictions for you to exercise and stretch your faith and love for God so that you can be prepared for eternity. Athletes who want to excel and succeed, accept their trainer's discipline, trusting in his expertise. You, too, will excel and succeed if you accept the Lord as your Savior and trust in His expertise. Your afflictions are the Lord's loving and often difficult lesson plans for you. Turn to Him and He will lift you through them. Alma said:

> *"Nevertheless, the Lord seeth fit to chasten his people; he trieth their patience and their faith. Nevertheless—whosoever putteth his trust in him the same shall be lifted up at the last day." (Mosiah 23:21-22)*

The Lord said:

"For he will give unto the faithful line upon line, precept upon precept; and I will try you and prove you herewith." (D&C 98:12)

"Therefore, they [the saints] must needs be chastened and tried, even as Abraham, who was commanded to offer up his only son." (D&C 101:4)

"My people must be tried in all things, that they may be prepared to receive the glory that I have for them, even the glory of Zion; and he that will not bear chastisement is not worthy of my kingdom." (D&C 136:31)

Elder Ronald E. Poelman discussed adversity and our divine purpose here on earth. He said:

"Adversity, or what we perceive to be adversity, enters into the life of every individual at various times and in various forms." [6]

This is a powerful insight—that you look at your tribulations and perceive them to be adversity and not a self-evaluation. You are not your temptations, your afflictions, nor your tribulations, any more than a runner is a torn ligament or sprained hamstring muscle. You are simply a child of God experiencing tribulation.

It's easy to see affliction as a curse rather than a blessing. I'm sure that's part of what Lehi and Sariah perceived as their sons failed to return with the brass plates. I'm sure that's part of what Jacob perceived when he learned that his son, Joseph had been eaten by a wild beast. I'm sure that's part of what Peter felt when he saw the Jesus crucified. But, Lehi eventually received his sons and the brass plates then came to inherit the promised land and avoided being destroyed when Jerusalem fell. Jacob and all his people were eventually saved when the famine struck and his son, Joseph was in position to save them. Jesus eventually resurrected and empowered the church and all mankind by having allowed his own life to end.

When tribulations first hit, we do tend to define them as adversity, rather than as a gift from a loving Savior to enhance our journey back to Him. Sometimes it's hard to handle tribulation well. I remember riding home on the school bus one day. I was twelve years old. A little girl sitting in front of me got up and exited the bus. Suddenly she cried out in horror. I looked out the window to see that her little dog got hit by a car that had to slam on its brakes to stop for the bus. Without hesitating, the girl knelt beside her furry friend and tried to comfort him (its back legs had been crushed). The dog, as most animals will do when injured, barked and snapped at his owner. She retreated from its reach, but stayed with the dog while it suffered then passed away in front of her.

Sad as it sounds, we sometimes bark and snap at our Savior when we go through afflictions. Although, Jesus does not deserve our harsh reaction, He endures it faithfully and loyally, never leaving our side (even if we persist in lashing out at him). Yes, like that little girl loved her dog, the Savior loves us greater than any emotional outburst can undo.

"What should I do? What is thy will for me? Wilt thou help me to bear these burdens?" These should well be the prayerful supplications you offer to the Lord when tribulations hit. Avoid asking "why" because the Lord already answered that for you—to bring to pass your immortality and eternal life. As the tribulation endures call upon the Lord to strengthen your resolve, to make your burdens seem light so that you can bear them. As the Lord promised Alma's imprisoned people who were heavily burdened and forbidden to pray by their wicked captors:

"And I will also ease the burdens which are put upon your shoulders, that even you cannot feel them upon your backs, even

while you are in bondage; and this will I do that ye may stand as witnesses for me hereafter, and that ye may know of a surety that I, the Lord God, do visit my people in their afflictions." (Mosiah 24:14)

Elder Poelman also said:

"The Lord's own way of preparing us to see Him as He is may well include the refining furnace of affliction, that we may 'offer sacrifice to him of a broken heart and a contrite spirit,' the promised reward being peace in this world, and eternal life in the world to come." (See D&C 59:8, 23)

Refining as a metaphor fits very well into the plan of salvation. A furnace burns hot enough and long enough to cleanse metals of their impurities. Metallurgists speak of "pure" gold and silver that have been refined to the highest industry standards. If we turn to the Lord during our refining process, we become purified. I once sat in Fast and Testimony meeting where a friend stood and bore his witness. Among other things, he said:

"I love the Lord. I could not make it without Him. All you here know of my recent struggles. Sometimes, I think I see the light at the end of the tunnel. Then as it draws closer I realize that it's just the furnace door, opening for more coal to be shoveled into my refining process."

This man endured immense suffering for years that drew him closer to the Savior and that brought his children along with him.

Elder Adhemar Damiani spoke of the meaning of life, tribulation, and happiness when he said:

"Why does life seem so difficult? Why does there seem to be so much sadness, hate, and unhappiness in the world? Why do the innocent suffer? Why are there so many unhappy

people? Many are unhappy because they do not know the plan of salvation; others do not believe the plan of salvation; and others, although they believe, are not willing to pay the price for happiness. Do you believe in the plan of salvation? Are you willing to pay the price?"

"Jacob described those who are willing to pay this price: 'Behold, the righteous, the saints of the Holy One of Israel, they who have believed in the Holy One of Israel, they who have endured the crosses of the world, and despised the shame of it, they shall inherit the kingdom of God, which was prepared for them from the foundation of the world, and their joy shall be full forever.' (2 Nephi 9:18)

"Our Heavenly Father wants each one of us to receive a fullness of His blessings. Will we become discouraged because of the adversaries of the world? No! Let us be optimistic. Let us have faith in the future, knowing that the plan of salvation is true. Let us trust the Father and endure to the end." [7]

President Joseph Fielding Smith talked about knowing the Father in whom we should place our trust. He said:

"God is our Father; he is the being in whose image man is created...he is the literal and personal father of the spirits of all men...we must believe in God as the possessor of the fullness of all these characteristics [omnipotent; omniscient; all powerful; all wise; all knowing; perfect; possessing all faith, knowledge, power, justice, judgement, mercy, and truth." [8]

From this moment forward consider yourself on a fantastic journey from the pre-mortal world to earth life and eventually far beyond which will one day end up in Heavenly Father's presence. Your all knowing, all powerful, all loving, and all merciful Father in Heaven designed this master plan so that your journey gives you every chance to come unto Him. And you will.

CHAPTER THREE

Know Your Divine Self

Your memory was veiled when you were born. That's why you don't remember who you really are. That's why sometimes you get confused about who you are. Who you really are exists independent of what you do and what your current status (marital, parenting, wealth, education, calling, or other) might or might not be.

Yes, it's true you may be a teacher, athlete, doctor, or cashier. But, that's not who you are—it's just what you do. Who you <u>really</u> are, first and foremost, is a child of your Heavenly Father. You are just as valuable to your Father in Heaven now as you were when you left His presence to come down to this earth. This simple truth of being God's child can be so powerful to you if witnessed in the depths of your soul.

I personally saw the sweet and empowering influence of knowing I am a child of God in 1983. I was a full-time missionary, serving in Marseille, France. I had stopped a young man on the street and introduced my companion and myself as missionaries. Of course we were looking for opportunities to teach the discussions. The young man appeared interested and told us he was a seminary student considering a life as a Catholic priest. I asked him if he would like to have us come and talk to his local class of seminary students. To my utter surprise he accepted the offer and asked if he could invite the nuns and priests also attending the seminary to attend. Before the brief encounter on the sidewalk ended, our district of elders and sisters was scheduled to talk to about 30 priests, nuns, and seminary students in one of the more prominent cathedrals of Marseille.

What an opportunity for us as missionaries! As a district we counseled about the impression we'd like to make and the message that we'd like to give. It was agreed that we would briefly introduce the church, trying to avoid any sensitive subjects that might lead to conflict. It was also agreed that we would sing a song for them.

We all met at the cathedral as planned. It stood about six stories tall inside with flying buttress architecture. We stood in front of the pews answering questions. But, the group seemed to be only mildly interested in who we were and what we had to say. I guessed that they already had studied a bit about the church. As the meeting ended, we sang these sacred words:

> *"I am a child of God,*
> *And he has sent me here,*
> *Has given me an earthly home*
> *With parents kind and dear.*
> *I am a child of God,*
> *And so my needs are great;*
> *Help me to understand his words*
> *Before it grows too late.*
> *I am a child of God,*
> *Rich blessings are in store;*
> *If I but learn to do his will*
> *I'll live with him once more.*
> *Lead me, guide me,*
> *walk beside me,*
> *Help me find the way.*
> *Teach me all that I must do*
> *To live with him someday."* [9]

Oh, if you could have been there to hear it sung in French! "Je suis enfant de Dieu," *I am a child of God*. Our combined voices resonated within the stone walls of the cathedral and the Holy Spirit bore witness to many in attendance of its simple, yet powerful truth. The tears flowed freely and smiles filled the faces of those listening to our message. We were graciously thanked for having come to speak and repeatedly complimented on the sweet song, with its sweet message of truth. For a brief moment the Holy Spirit bore witness in such a way that religious differences didn't matter.

You too, must come to feel the witness of your true Heavenly parentage and come to know for yourself if this truth is to be of any use to you. Understanding it in your mind is not enough. This truth needs to be felt in your heart and known like any aspect of your testimony is known, in every fiber of your being. In the Bible Dictionary under the topic of "Prayer," you can read about your true relationship to God:

> "*As soon as we learn the true relationship in which we stand toward God (namely, God is our Father, and we are his children), then at once prayer becomes natural and instinctive on our part (Matt. 7:7-11). Many of the so-called difficulties about prayer arise from forgetting this relationship. Prayer is the act by which the will of the Father and the will of the child are brought into correspondence with each other. The object of prayer is not to change the will of God, but to secure for ourselves and for others blessings that God is already willing to grant, but that are made conditional on our asking for them. Blessings require some work or effort on our part before we can obtain them. Prayer is a form of work, and is an appointed means for obtaining the highest of all blessings.*"

Feeling in your heart that you are a child of God comes through your prayerful efforts. Prayer is a form of work that secures desired blessings from Heavenly Father. In fact, my most powerful experience with this truth came a few years prior to my full-mission. I struggled through my adolescent years. As a teenager, everything in my life felt wrong, out of place, and awkward. My step-mother had seen my struggles. One day, she urged me to find a peace within myself that would be strong enough to overcome the doubt and trouble in my soul.

I followed her specific suggestions and in the summer of my fifteenth year, every night I prayed, kneeling beside my bed, "Please, Lord. Help me to know that I am a child of God. Help me to feel in my heart who I really am." Gradually, over the course of that summer, it settled into my soul. My inspired step-mother was right. With the witness of my divine birthright growing in my heart and soul, came a peace that enabled me to cope with the doubt and trouble of my adolescent development. I came to know in such a profound way that I have a Father in Heaven who loved me before my earthly parents were even born. He knows me, loves me, guides my life, protects me, and cares for me. His attention to me never wanders, never sleeps, never gets distracted, and never fails to respond to my prayers. Heavenly Father is really there and really answers every child's prayer. These facts can be known by you, too. Have you prayerfully asked the Lord to gain your own testimony of your own divine self?

President Gordon B. Hinckley gave a sweet talk that was recently included in the *Friend* magazine. In it he said:

> *"Never forget, my dear young friends, that you really are a child of God who has inherited something of His divine nature, one whom He loves and desires to help and bless. I pray that our Heavenly Father will bless you. May He smile with favor upon you. May you walk in His paths and follow His teachings. May you ever be prayerful unto Him, praying always in the name of His Beloved Son, the Lord Jesus Christ. May each of us*

resolve to always follow Him in faith. May life be kind to you, for you are indeed a child of God, worthy and deserving of His love and blessing. It is not asking too much, is it, to take a few minutes of each day to speak with your Father in Heaven when you know that you are a child of God?" [10]

You are a child of God! You were literally born of a Heavenly Father and Mother before you came to this earth to your mortal parents. You have a Divine birthright that sets you apart from all of God's other creations and that entitles you to the most important gift that God has ever given to mankind—the gift of the Atonement of Jesus Christ.

Before time began, you proved yourself among the valiant of God's many children. You chose the plan of salvation over the opposing more worldly plan. Your very presence here as a mortal testifies to your valiant nature. You also came with exceptional personal spiritual qualities which enabled you to embrace the gospel of Jesus Christ when you heard it and to continue onward, again choosing the Father's plan over other more worldly alternatives.

Think about the statistical probabilities of being a member of God's true church on the earth today. There are well over 6.5 billion people living on this planet and only 12 million members. In spite of the existence of these vast numbers, there is still only one of you. And you are intimately known to your Heavenly Father and to Jesus Christ.

Yes, the numbers of God's children appear to be countless to us. But I say again, you are known to the Lord. The Book of Moses shows us that the Lord knows all the inhabitants of this world.

In fact, he showed Moses all the inhabitants of this earth. (In Ether 3:25 you can read that he also showed them to the Brother of Jared). To Moses, He explained that they are innumerable unto man *"but all things are numbered unto me, for they are mine, and I know them." (Moses 1:35)* Because Moses knew his divine nature he resisted Satan when confronted face-to-face, ultimately calling upon the name of Jesus Christ to cast Satan out. (See Moses 1.)

You can be intimately known to Heavenly Father even though you are not His only child. For example, you have more than one niece, nephew, child, grandchild, or friend. You know them all. If you were allowed to have your full intelligence at your disposal (not just the veiled intelligence we get while in mortality), you'd be able to know and love them even more than you do now.

It is confusing for us at times because we only have a finite intelligence while our Father in Heaven and Jesus Christ have infinite intelligence (they are simply much, much smarter than us). Jesus knows the worlds he has created, all the inhabitants thereon, and even the number of hairs on our head, *"But even the very hairs of your head are numbered." (Luke 12:7)*

You just have to accept on faith that he personally knows and loves you as He does each of the billions of others. Sing for it, pray for it, fast for it and act as though it is true. Eventually it will distill upon your soul as does the dews from heaven . . . you are a child of God!

CHAPTER FOUR

Learn To Trust Again: Atonement Therapy

The Fourth Article of Faith reads, *"We believe that the first principles and ordinances of the gospel are: first, Faith in the Lord Jesus Christ; second, Repentance . . ."* No man or woman can learn to trust again after having been hurt, unless he or she has faith that Jesus can heal and can forgive us. You see, that great plan of salvation which rests on three pillars (the creation, the fall, and the Atonement) made a way in advance for you to heal when injured.

Jesus himself was the leader in all three of these major undertakings. Jesus agreed to save you from death and sin. You chose to assist in the creation. You must also choose to receive the Atonement.

Some still struggle with the issue of vast numbers of God's children when it comes to understanding the Atonement. They ask, "How can Jesus atone for me when he died and suffered for so many others?" The answer is found in the scriptures. Isaiah speaks messianically when he declares:

> *"Behold, I have graven thee upon the palms of my hands; thy walls are continually before me." (Isaiah 49:16)*

Where might the Lord have been when he engraved you upon

the palms of his hands? He was in the Garden and on the cross. You see as He suffered all the pains and sorrows, He did it for each of you intimately. Every pain, discomfort, heartache, grief, and hurt you've ever experienced, he suffered. And not just once, but twice.[11]

Christ suffered in the Garden of Gethsemane, fulfilling all the demands that justice could met out upon him. Then he suffered them all again while hanging upon the cross on the Mount called Golgotha. He engraved your name upon his hands while He hurt your hurts and grieved your grief. The walls that tend to stop you in your tracks, He also faced then climbed. He and He alone can help you surmount your walls because He has already successfully surmounted them.

Jesus suffered for us all—one at a time until billions had been atoned for—so that He can know how to succor you, to heal you, to save you when you seek His help during the difficult times of your mortal probation. He is the only one who can.

True, your friends, family, therapist, home and visiting teacher, bishop, or stake president can counsel and advise. But, their counsel and advice won't and can't save you. At very best, it can direct you to the source that can save you. Your only hope is through the Atonement of Jesus Christ. Below is the same diagram shown previously of your path to surrender. It's also a diagram of your path to the healing power of the Atonement.

You → Jesus → Heavenly Father

Imagine with me for a moment that you've gone to the Holy Land to visit the sacred sights there. Exhausted from the long journey you retire to your hotel room, kneel to pray, and fall quickly asleep. Somehow, in a dream or vision you discover that you've gone back through time to the end of Christ's life. You walk out into the market, not understanding a word spoken by the local citizens. You search through the streets for hours, unable to ask for help. Your deepest desire is to seek the Lord and ask Him to help you back. At the end of one street that ascends to the edge of the city, you see a man hanging on a cross. You run with all haste climbing stairs until you reach the mount called Golgotha. Somehow you muster the courage to look upon the contorted frame of the pitiful man on the cross. He isn't Jesus.

You flee the hillside of death, not knowing it was adorned by the jagged rocks that resemble a human skull. Soon you run past a burial tomb. The large round door laying to the side reminds you that Christ is no longer here.

You eventually find your self walking alone on a dry road. The sign reads "Emmaus." Hours later, you realize that He will not walk this way now. Suddenly you find yourself outside the Wall of Jerusalem. You recognize this garden, the hip-level boulder beneath the olive tree.

"Gethsemane," you whisper. You wait and wait for the Savior to come. Hours pass. Finally in desperation, you kneel down and pray.

"Heavenly Father," you whisper, hoping He hears you. "Thank thee for all I have been blessed with. Thank thee for thy Son, Jesus Christ and this sacred land where he fulfilled his mortal mission. Father, I am lost. I need the help of my Savior, have Him heal me, and help me find my way back."

"I'm here." A peaceful feeling enters your heart.

You open your eyes to discover yourself, kneeling in your hotel room, beside your own bed.

I'm always right here. The message burns deep within your heart.

"Thank you," you reply with tears overflowing. You thumb through your things to find the picture of Christ you brought with you. His eyes appear to look deeply into yours. Peace fills your heart as you realize that you don't need to go anywhere other than your own bedroom, car, desk, or yard to find the healing influence of the Savior. Even in the Holy Land He comes to you. All you must do is believe, have faith, then ask in prayer, wherever you are at the time, addressing your Heavenly Father, thanking him for your blessings, and asking for your Saviors' assistance before you close in Jesus Christ's name. It really is that simple.

There are some who erroneously turn to other mortals for healing, misunderstanding the power of the Atonement and underestimating the mercy of the Lord. Be cautious not to let this be your diagram.

You → another mortal → Heavenly Father

That means to be wary of seeking the Atonement from your friends, family, therapist, home or visiting teacher, bishop, or stake president. Seek their help in finding Christ. But, once you find Him, directly entreat Him for His all powerful, eternal and infinite healing power.

So, how? What must you do to become one who can fully utilize the Atonement of Christ? Blessings do require some effort on our part before we can receive them. Read the Savior's invitation in the following two verses:

"Come unto me, all ye that labour and are heavy laden, and I will give you rest." (Matthew 11:28)

"He inviteth them all to come unto him and partake of his goodness; and he denieth none that come unto him, black and white, bond and free, male and female; and he remembereth the heathen; and all are alike unto God, both Jew and Gentile." (2 Nephi 26:33)

Please notice that Jesus extended his invitation to "all" He didn't say come unto me only ye that are perfect, or perfectly stationed in life, or without need of healing.

On that latter subject he said in Moroni 8:8:

"Listen to the words of Christ, your redeemer, your Lord and your God. Behold I came to the world not to call the righteous but sinners to repentance; the whole need no physician, but they that are sick."

When you call upon the Savior's Atonement, think of it as though it were like a hospital. Picture the information sign that might sit in the entrance to the hospital foyer. Obviously the deeper you journey with Christ into "Atonement General Hospital" the more significant the blessing to you. You'll never find a cashier in this place. All that is required is your faith and willful desire to enter. You'll also discover that the Atonement is not in a geographic place or specific building (although you may feel it's healing power in the temples, sacrament meetings, and homes).

Some misunderstand the availability of the Atonement in their lives. They erroneously think that they might somehow overburden their Savior. As if Jesus were just another ward member or friend who's already too traumatized to help them in their suffering. This truly is a mistaken idea.

You have to do more than just know about the Atonement. You have to have faith in the great plan of salvation, faith in your Heavenly Father, faith in Jesus Christ, and faith that Jesus suffered an infinite and eternal atonement which covers everything essential to your exaltation.

How?

Simple, our Heavenly Father is all-knowing and all-powerful. He knew in advance of the Atonement, all that would be required to heal all your wounds and pay all your debts of sin. When Jesus went through the actual agonies of the Atonement—thousands of years before you were even born—He covered everything you'd ever need from Him. Everything!

WELCOME TO ATONEMENT GENERAL HOSPITAL

First Floor

At-one-ment Services—signing you up to partner with and become one with Christ

Friendship Services—rediscovering your friendship with Christ

Counseling Services—empathetic listening from one who has been there

Pain Relief Services—immediate comfort during suffering

Transport Services—assistance with carrying burdens

Integrity Maintenance Services—continuity in your divine nature

Resistence Services—immunization against evil

Revelation Services—answers to personal dilemmas

Divine Awareness Services—recognizing the goodness of Christ

Extraction Services—Forgiveness and removal of your sins

Second Floor

Infusion Services—hope and faith lifts

Surrender Services—transferring your infirmities and sicknesses to Christ

Maintenance Service—strengthening your shoulders to carry long-term heavy burdens

Transformation Service—natural man tendency removal

Wound Repair Services—healing deep emotional and spiritual wounds

Physical Health Services—healing physical maladies

Poison Control Services—assistance with forgiving offenders

Grafting Services—joining your will to the Lord's

Outreach Services—bringing others to Christ

Third Floor

Redemption Services—mediation to Heavenly Father

Purification and Refinement Services—please bring your tribulations with you

Endurance Services—long-lasting support leading to your salvation and exaltation

Sanctification Services—please bring service and afflictions with you

Reconciliation Services—grace unto justification

Resurrection and Judgment Services— by appointment only

It is impossible to over burden the Lord. It's like the guy who slipped on the ice and landed hard on his forearm. He stubbornly waited two weeks before the pain finally forced him to go into the Doctor's office. When the doctor explained to the man that he had fractured both arm bones in his lower arm, he asked why the man waited so long to come in for medical help.

"I knew how busy you were and didn't want to bother you," the man explained.

"But, I'm a doctor. It's what I do. It's my job," the doctor replied.

Jesus clearly invites you and me, especially since we "labour and are heavy laden," come to Him now, not later. Think about who Jesus is and why and how he is qualified to make such an invitation. He is the Savior of mankind. He finished His ministry upon this earth and finished His ultimate life's mission to atone for and save mankind. Like the highly skilled physicians of our day who advertise their surgical skills to us, Jesus advertises his unique and divine expertise to you.

Jesus heals with the same availability that we find in emergency rooms. You can walk in any time, night or day. The difference between Jesus and the emergency room is that you never have to pay, there's never a waiting line, and you don't have travel from where you are to seek Jesus' help. He's like the ER that comes to you. You can call upon him from your car, your closet, your workplace, anywhere.

But, you do have to seek him out, the same as the man who fell had to seek out the doctor. Seeking out Jesus' time and energy in our healing process requires work on our part—our willful desire to have him be a part of our lives. John the Revelator declared:

"Behold, I stand at the door, and knock: if any man hear my voice, and open the door, I will come into him, and will sup with him and he with me." (Revelation 3:20)

I love the wording chosen in this scripture. Jesus promises that if you'll open the door, then he'll "sup" with you. When our friends sit at the table in our home, we not only eat, but we visit, we solve the world's problems, we share our faith and hope, we listen to each other's lamentations, and we create emotional ties that strengthen us to keep on going.

Don't you do the same? Wouldn't it be wonderful to literally have the Savior at your table, to offer up your pains and sorrow unto him, to hear him express his understanding of what you've been through and how He too suffered the same exact thing! Jesus wants to heal your broken heart, bind up your wounds, and restore the trust you lost in the wake of your affliction. In 3 Nephi 9:13, Jesus invites:

> *"O all ye that are spared because ye were more righteous than they, will ye not now return unto me..."*

In this scripture, Jesus is speaking to those who survived the calamities in the Americas just before He visited them. They are sitting in a vapor of darkness so thick that a fire can't be started. What a beautiful metaphor of being called from darkness into the light of Christ! And you're not just invited to come and meet him as two strangers might meet. Jesus knew you before your mortal probation. He remembers your friendship even if you don't. He invites you to "return to him."

Coming to Christ is a renewal of existing friendship bonds. He continues through the rest of verse 13 and 14:

> *"...will ye not now return unto me, and repent of your sins, and be converted, that I may heal you? Yea, verily I say unto you, if ye will come unto me ye shall have eternal life. Behold mine arm of mercy is extended towards you, and whosoever will come, him will I receive; and blessed are those who come unto me."*

As you return, you are promised repentance, conversion, healing, and ultimately eternal life. Jesus invites you, with His extended arms of mercy. Elder Henry B. Eyring said that he knew that his mother loved the Savior and understood her relationship with him:

> *"She knew the Savior, and she loved Him. I had learned from her that we do not close in the name of a stranger when we approach our Father in prayer."* [12]

Jesus is a friend not a stranger, a healer not an administrator, and lover of your soul not a ruler. Do you believe this for yourself?

I can testify that he will receive you with mercy and healing. I struggled for years in the way I saw Jesus and Heavenly Father in my prayers. Before, when I prayed I saw Heavenly Father on a large golden throne sitting on the other side of a large mountain in such a way that I knew He was there, but could not approach Him. As I studied the issue I came to realize that it was my perception and experience of patriarchal figures that led me to see Heavenly Father this way. It was my problem.

So, in my early 30s I began to pray often to be able to see him as a personage in front of me, close to me. I soon became ill and suffered pains that hurt 24 hours a day, seven days a week, for nearly six months. Test after test and antibiotic after antibiotic failed to find or cure the problem. I received a priesthood blessing from my bishop. Shortly thereafter, an ultrasound indicated a golf ball sized tumor (later identified as being benign). The day before my scheduled surgery, a second ultrasound found no tumor at all, but my pain persisted. (I didn't know it at the time but the ultrasound technician was different the second time and there was some sort of mix up in the orders.) But when I heard the report stating that there was no tumor, I felt that it had invalidated all my suffering and left me back at the starting point for finding out what caused the pain and where it had come from.

I came home from the doctor's office and got out the lawn mower. I cut the grass on a 100-degree, sunny July day. I felt so angry and betrayed. At one point while I pushed the mower across the yard, I began to add up all that I had been through over the last six months, then the years before that, then my entire life. I became angrier and angrier. In my heart, I imagined that I was speaking to the Lord and I expressed blame to Him for what He had put me through.

Immediately after having blamed Him, the still small voice whispered to me that of all the people in my life, Jesus had been and was the one loyal friend who had never hurt me, never betrayed me, and never let me down. I turned the mower around to make another pass through the yard. I felt so ashamed. I felt sorrow from my head to my toes. I had just accused my Savior and yet, I realized He was innocent.

I prayed asking Him to please forgive me. In an instant, before I was able to finish my prayer of repentance, I felt a feeling of His love embrace me. I felt his arms of mercy wrapped around me. I knew at that moment that He understood what I had been through. I felt his total forgiveness. But most importantly, for the first time in my life, I felt His very personal expression of love to me as I continued to cut the grass. In my feeble prayer, I expressed my gratitude for all that I had been blessed with. I thanked the Lord for his love. The next day, I had the tumor removed in a successful operation that ended the pain.

My friend later told me that he had driven past the house about the same time I cut the grass. He saw me soaked in perspiration, red-faced from the heat, and crying like a baby while I pushed the mower. He said he wanted to stop, but felt that he shouldn't at that time. I wanted to tell him then but, didn't know how, that I had made a great discovery. I knew that Jesus loves me personally. He knows my heart and my soul. He cares for me intimately.

He healed me personally. I am so grateful for tumors and other illnesses. To date, I've had eight major surgeries. Not only do I still feel my Savior's personal love for me when I pray, but now my Heavenly Father sits before me—I at his feet—and my Savior stands (as he literally and figuratively always has) beside me with his hand on my shoulder.

You see, I had forgotten that I was not alone in my mortal sojourn. Jesus reminded me and continues to do so in the current pains I suffer. Like you, I, too, have suffered many pains of body and soul. I am so grateful for them. They turn me toward my Savior. And that is where the blessing of learning to trust again is found—in turning toward our Savior in our sorrow.

The blessing in the hurt, sorrow, pain, grief, loss, and humiliation comes because, these obstacles exceed our mortal abilities to cope with them. They help us to turn our hearts to the Savior for relief. Once in His arms of mercy, we gain a sure witness of His love for us.

Jesus wants us to seek him. He's given us trials to help turn our attention to him. The trials you have been given are a gift to you. (Yes, I did say a gift.) Eternal life is promised in 3 Nephi 9:14 and in Moses 1:39. What is "Eternal Life"? How does it relate to learning to trust again after we've been hurt? Why is having our trust violated really a great opportunity for us?

In John 17:3 we read:

"And this is life eternal, that they might know thee the only true God, and Jesus Christ, whom thou hast sent."

The verb, to know, is used in many different ways throughout the scriptures. It means to understand, to comprehend, to perceive. It's also used to mean—to be close to, to be intimate with, and to be friends with. Eternal life is to be like and to relate to our Heavenly Father and Jesus Christ. Eternal life is to live with them as they live and do with them as they "bring to pass the immortality and eternal life of man." Eternal life is an endless journey of progression. Our afflictions, in turning us to Jesus Christ help us to become like Him and our Heavenly Father. Look at this triangle:

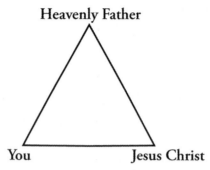

By approaching Jesus, you become healed and closer to Him. The more you draw unto Him the more you become like him, taking even His image in your countenances. And the more you become like him the higher you move up this triangle and the closer you come to know and become like our Heavenly Father. If you endure in your love of the Savior, eventually he will succeed in His work to bring to pass your personal immortality and eternal life. Then the triangle looks more and more like this:

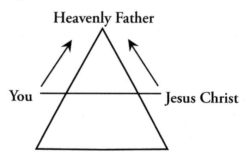

The Savior invites you to *"take his yoke upon you for his yoke is easy and his burden is light."* (*Matthew 11:29*) A yoke is a harness worn shoulder to shoulder between two draft animals (such as oxen and horses). They typically are placed side by side in the yoke only if they are about the same size. Otherwise, one pulls much more strongly than the other and it is ineffective.

However, in the case of Jesus' invitation He is asking you to yoke or join yourself to him—shoulder to shoulder—and have Him lead you back to your Heavenly Father. His Atonement and love compensate for your weaker strength next to Him. He carries His load and much of your load. You simply have to choose to "take His yoke upon you" and thereafter act in accordance with that choice.

Have you ever heard of a concept called "cellular honesty"? Cells are the smallest building block of the body. Millions and millions of them add up to comprise our body. When you have honest feelings, honest needs, honest concerns, honest fears, and honest expressions they add up to comprise cellular honesty.

You do have real needs, wants, feelings, and a real sense of who you are—your self. As you interact with others and express cellular honesty, you speak from the reality of your soul. The honesty at this level cannot be argued with, denied by others, nor invalidated by others. Some people describe cellular honesty as "soul talk." Interaction at this level takes practice, but is well worth the effort because it's the ultimate in intimate expression and if reciprocated leads to cellular relationships.

Soul talk is speaking without any justification, defense, or excuse. It is 100 percent legitimate and it assumes the greatest trust on the part of the listener. I can only recommend one person to you for this level of microscopic soul talk—Jesus Christ. He alone represents the undeniable 100 percent trustworthy listener. He alone will listen without injury to you. He will respond without selfishness toward you. He will answer you with your exaltation in mind. He is trustworthy.

To learn to trust again is to come unto Jesus Christ, praying for support in your ability to express your cellular soul-felt needs, wants, and concerns. This requires much faith (back to the Fourth Article of Faith again). It also requires repentance. When we've been hurt we need to repent if:

1) offense was taken

2) retaliation transpired

3) our human or "natural man" qualities added to the hurt

In any human interaction each person bears some measure of responsibility (even if only 99.99 percent on the offender and 0.01 percent on his or her victim). Once you've asked for forgiveness for yourself you need to ask forgiveness for the offender. Jesus taught in 3 Nephi 12:44-45:

> *"But behold I say unto you, bless them that curse you, do good to them that hate you, and pray for them who despitefully use you and persecute you; That ye may be the children of your Father who is in Heaven; for He maketh the sun to rise on the evil and the good."*

There is a cleansing process that comes when you do good to your offenders (even if you only pray for blessings upon them). The cleansing is within you. President Spencer W. Kimball taught:

> *"To forgive one who is mean and offensive is the act of one near to perfection."* [13]

You must cast those burdens of being offended upon your Savior and yoke yourself to Him to be healed.

Forgiveness is essential to learning to trust again.

Forgiveness stops the offense from creating echo offenses—pains and hurt from memories and scars—even if you have to ask for forgiveness every single day for the next ten years. We often hear of groups of survivors like "survivors of 9/11, survivors of the attack on Pearl Harbor, survivors of the Columbine High school shooting." Now, listen to how it sounds if we replace survivor with the word victim: "victims of 9/11, victims of the attack on Pearl Harbor, victims of the Columbine High School shooting." The word "victim" by definition implies having been cheated, fooled, or taken advantage of on purpose or by accident. The word "survivor" implies by definition having outlasted the trauma, having stayed alive, having been spared. Victims are entitled to reparation, survivors just "keep on trucking" in spite of their traumas. Surviving is often a conscious act on the part of those who've been traumatized. They decide to let the past go, to retire from being a victim, to move on with the best of their abilities, and to forgive and as much as possible forget the offenses.

Asking for your forgiveness and that of your offender may take more faith than you feel you now have. This is where you follow the example given in Mark 9:23-24:

"Jesus said unto him, if thou canst believe, all things are possible to him that believeth. And straightway the father of the child cried out, and said with tears, Lord I believe, help thou mine unbelief."

This story was about a man desiring a healing of his own child. The Savior did strengthen the man's unbelief and heal the child. Ask for the same blessing for yourself. Pray for the Lord to strengthen your unbelief and to do so at the cellular and soul-level. In so doing, you'll invoke the power of the Atonement to help you receive its healing power. There is not a man nor woman on this earth that can live a perfect enough life to save him or herself. All of us are sinners. Jesus calls us in this fallen state to come to Him. Elder Eyring also said:

"But there is one need the hardened and proud person cannot believe they can meet for themselves. They cannot lift the weight of sin from their own shoulders."

I don't use this scripture to sound discouraging. I use it to sound precise in helping you to come unto Christ and know the true nature of your relationship to Him. Elder Eyring spoke of Alma, who preached to his own son:

"O my son, I desire that ye should deny the justice of God no more. Do not endeavor to excuse yourself in the least point because of your sins, by denying the justice of God; but do you let the justice of God, and his mercy, and his long-suffering have full sway in your heart; and let it bring you down to the dust in humility." (Alma 42:30)

The process of you learning to trust takes place in humility (a knowledge of your fallen or natural state as a mortal), in prayer (an effort from one who is dependent upon the Lord), in prayerful meditation at home and at sacrament meeting, and in the temple (acts of faith and works). Elder James E. Faust said,

"For many of us, however, spiritual healing takes place not in the great arenas of the world but in our sacrament meetings. It is comforting to worship with, partake of the sacrament with, and be taught in the spirit of humility by neighbors and close friends who love the Lord and try to keep His commandments. Our sacrament meetings should be worshipful and healing... through music...through bearing and hearing humble testimonies." [14]

After the attacks of September 11, 2001, I found myself in sacrament meeting, singing the sacrament hymn. My eyes filled with tears as I prayed for the Lord to relieve me of the deep sense of loss for all those injured and killed persons and their family and friends. Peace came to my heart as I literally partook of the bread and water. I gained more solace by listening to the talks and singing other hymns during that meeting than I had in any other one.

Visualize this as you seek prayerful healing. Imagine that you're on a hike. Your grief is like rotten food, your sorrows like poison, your hurts like heavy chunks of rusty steel. You pack your grief, sorrows, and hurts in the backpack and sling it across your shoulders. You hike across the barren terrain of Jerusalem until you happen upon a garden near the old city wall. You enter to find your Savior there, praying aloud and mentioning your name in His prayers.

"Jesus." You whisper and walk up to where He kneels and kneel beside Him.

He looks up from the ground, His eyes meeting yours. He extends His hand, gesturing for your backpack. You remove the backpack and hand it to Him. He places it on his shoulders, smiles at you, then returns to His prayers. The longer He prays, the smaller your Backpack appears until it finally disappears altogether.

"Thank you." You say as you rise to your feet and walk out of the garden. A few feet away you turn to take one last look. You see another entering the garden with a backpack twice as large as your's once was. Have faith that Jesus can and will do this for you. Believe that He can and He will.

I testify to you that when you call upon the Savior's Atonement, a cleansing will come and it will restore your ability to trust again. But, most important, you will know how much your Savior loves you. You will know for yourself of His unwavering devotion to everything that brings you back to your Heavenly Father. You will know of Jesus' personality and nature and then you will know of Heavenly Father's. For they are one in purpose and love.

Since your afflictions (injuries) bring you to humble yourself and turn to the Lord, they are in fact a gift to you. In the New Testament, Paul discusses how the Lord gives men weaknesses that they might triumph over them and thereby gain strength in the Lord. Paul said:

> "Therefore I take pleasure in infirmities, in reproaches, in necessities, in persecutions, in distresses for Christ sake: for when I am weak, then am I strong." (2 Cor. 12:10)

Paul did suffer adversity, persecution, and humiliation great and small. He rejoiced in them because he took them to the Lord for a healing. What type of attitude did Paul have, given that his history included being: a fugitive as a saint, tried in courts, shipwrecked, snake bit, imprisoned, starved, neglected, humiliated and ultimately martyred for the cause? Paul's attitude is described in an epistle to the Philippians 4:11-13:

> *"Not that I speak in respect of want: for I have learned, in whatsoever state I am, therewith to be content. I know both how to be abased, and I know how to abound: every where and in all things I am instructed both to be full and to be hungry, both to abound and to suffer need. I can do all things through Christ which strengtheneth me."*

Paul found peace in his mortal probation because he allowed his sufferings to turn him to the Lord. What do you allow your sufferings to do for you? In the Book of Ether we gain more insight into where weaknesses come from and what the Lord expects us to do with them. Ether 12:27 reads:

> *"And if men come unto me I will show unto them their weakness. I give unto men weakness that they may be humble; and my grace is sufficient for all men that humble themselves before me; for if they humble themselves before me, and have faith in me, then will I make weak things become strong unto them."*

This verse teaches you so much about the nature of Jesus Christ as your teacher and Savior. He gives you weaknesses. Yes, even weaknesses that contribute in part to the difficult circumstances you often find yourself in.

All of us, you and me included, are mortals and "prone to wander . . . prone to leave the God I love," as the song *Come Thou Fount of Every Blessing* says. You and I can and should choose the same type of attitude that Paul chose, to be *"content in whatsoever state you are in."*

Simply put, you will suffer (more than you already have). And if you want to align yourself to the Lord's will in your life, it is best to gratefully accept those difficult trials that you can't change as an opportunity to grow, to learn, and most importantly to better know your personal Savior, the Lord Jesus Christ. Utilizing the Atonement is crucial in learning to trust again. So, too, is serving others.

Chapter Five

Know God Through Service to Others

Have you ever found yourself praying, "Help me to finish this day, Lord. I'm exhausted." And you're saying this prayer at 10:00 am? As part of our mortal probation, you and I have finite daily strength and energy. Many days the demands placed upon us exceed our energy available to meet them. For years, therapists and authors of self-help books have used the metaphor of a well to describe our emotional reserves. The metaphor is as follows: we each have a well which requires our daily attention to be filled. If our well is full we have enough to share with others. If it is very empty we can't draw from it to fill our own needs much less the needs of others. This metaphor fits the real-world that most of us live in. We regularly need to slow down, rest, and refill our wells, so that we have enough to give to others.

Jesus was the same way. He could even feel when virtue had *"gone out"* from him when a woman was healed who touched the hem of his robe (Matthew 9:20-22). He knew when water had been drawn from his well's reserve. He also knew He had to, at times, replenish His reserves. Jesus set an example of this before He began his ministry. He'd fasted and retreated to the wilderness to *"be with God." (Matthew 4:1 JST)*

Later, Jesus calmed the stormy seas when he exclaimed *"peace be still."* (Mark 4:38-39) He felt secure enough that he had been asleep on a pillow in the hinder part of the ship.

At various times Jesus chose to be alone. John 6:15 reads:

> *"When Jesus therefore perceived that they would come and take him by force, to make him a king, he departed again into a mountain himself alone."*

While on the brink of the most difficult task of His life's mission in Gethsemane, Jesus told his disciples, *"...sit ye here, while I go pray yonder."* (Matthew 26:36) They did and He did. Even after His resurrection, while in the Americas, Jesus withdrew from the people to pray alone:

> *"and it came to pass that Jesus departed out of the midst of them, and went a little way off from them and bowed himself to the earth..."* (3 Nephi 19:19)

Interestingly, most of our scriptural accounts about Jesus are about his giving, serving, and doing for others. Even when He was exhausted and the disciples tried to protect Him from children who wanted to spend time with Him. Jesus allowed the little children to come unto Him, and *". . . he laid his hands on them, and departed thence."* (Matthew 19:13-14)

Jesus filled his well because He spent most of His ministry in service to others and regularly called upon His reserves. For example, in His short three-year ministry we have recorded that He: healed the sick, raised the dead, taught, performed miracles, spent time with his family and friends, cast out devils, proclaimed His mission from His Father, called sinners to repentance, forgave, reproved, attended feasts and marriages.

The Savior also traveled, fulfilled all prophecies about His ministry, instituted the sacrament, set up the Church and its leadership, performed the Atonement, and surrendered His life.

There are probably many other events He was a part of that were not recorded in the New Testament, but the lesson is clear—we must regularly take some time to fill our own wells, because most of our daily lives involve service to others. Therein lies a key to knowing God—we daily fill our spiritual wells and daily serve those around us. Elder Bernard P. Brockbank wrote an *Ensign* article wherein he explained:

> *"The Lord has indicated that the gates of hell cannot prevail against revelation from him to any one of his children who desires to know the living God and to know the living Jesus Christ. This is available by divine commitment and by divine will, that for anyone desiring to know God the Eternal Father and to know his son Jesus Christ, God is under commitment and the gates of hell cannot prevail against that commitment; and it will be revealed through the power and principle of revelation direct from God to the one desiring to receive that information."* [15]

The promise is clear. If you desire to know God it cannot be held from you. Elder Brockbank lays out the principles of how to know God. He taught that to know God we must: believe in Him (not just know about Him); keep His commandments; stay close to the Church and its teachings (in activity and service to others); study the scriptures; and learn of Christ and follow His example.

Jesus taught us to love and serve God and our fellow man. He personally taught this in word and example and He inspired His chosen Prophets to teach us. *"That ye love one another, as I have loved you"* (John 13:34). Parents were also instructed:

> *"But ye will teach them [your children] to walk in the ways of truth and soberness; ye will teach them to love one another, and to serve one another."* (Mosiah 4:15)

The scriptures also teach:

"And we know also that sanctification through our Lord and Savior Jesus Christ is just and true, to all those who love and serve God with all of their mights, minds, and strength." (D & C 20:31)

"If thou lovest me thou shalt serve me and keep all of my commandments." (D & C 42:29)

President Gordon B. Hinckley taught:

"There are so many out there who need you. There are so many other people and causes out there who need your help. I'm not suggesting you become a Florence Nightingale or a Clara Barton, but you can help. The best antidote for worry is work. The best medicine for despair is service. The best cure for weariness is the challenge of helping someone who is even more tired." [16]

It's much easier to serve when you know others need your service. It is also much more rewarding and renewing as well as difficult and demanding to serve when you feel that nothing is left in your reserves. Most who serve (when only vapors remain in their wells) find themselves filled with Christ's love during and after their service. The Greeks called it Agapé (pronounced *ah-ga-pay*) love. Others call it selfless love. Christ simply called it charity, or the pure love of Christ. (See 1 Corinthians 13.)

Why love and service? How do these two actions fill our wells? As is mentioned above, sanctification comes to all those who love and serve God with all their mights, minds, and strength. This became clear to me once while in a stake priesthood training meeting. During the question and answer period, I asked a visiting authority about what we should do when there is so much demanded of us and we are so tired.

I really don't even remember the visiting authority's name,

but I've always remembered the principle he taught us that day. Basically, when we are tired, exhausted, rundown, and feel that we can't do any more, yet we do more out of love for God, then we are renewed by the Holy Spirit. This renewal is a form of being sanctified, where our wells are replenished far beyond explanation.

After hearing this explanation, the light bulb came on for me. I remembered how many times I had gone home teaching, awakened hours before church to attend meetings, stayed up late helping a neighbor in need, been awakened in the middle of the night to bless a sick child, gone to the hospital to attend to a sick friend, or attended the temple during ward temple night only to discover the sweet and undeniable feeling of renewal and overall refreshment to body and soul.

All throughout the remainder of each day I had given service and sometimes through to the next, my worries disappeared or became defined in a more manageable way. The fatigue disappeared. And at times the crises resolved themselves through divine intervention.

The Lord even watches over your family and friends while you serve. A few years ago, my wife Alisa and I drove from Springville, Utah, to Rexburg, Idaho, so that she could attend and I could teach at the BYU-Idaho Education Week. By the end of the four-days worth of sunup to sundown socializing, lectures, and activities we seriously considered the possibility of staying another night just to rest and recover.

But, each of us had church responsibilities we wanted to fulfill the next day. We chose to drive home even though tired. On the way home, about two hours from our Springville exit, while driving south on I-15, the Holy Spirit whispered to me. I called home and asked my young adult niece (who had stayed with our six children while we traveled) specifically to speak to our youngest child, Abraham. While I waited on the phone, my niece went down stairs to get him, because he had been watching a video in the family room.

She returned to say that Abraham wasn't there but if I wanted to talk to another child, she'd eventually find Abraham. I felt strongly, again by the Holy Spirit, to have her find Abraham right then. She sat the phone down and searched the entire house and yard. She came back and tearfully reported that he was gone!

She asked us to call back five minutes later while she and the other children split up and searched both sides of the neighborhood to see if he had snuck away to a friend's home. We hung up, looked at each other and realized that Abraham was in the hands of the Lord. We could not call anyone at this time of day to get help. We could not be there nor speed any faster to get home in time to intervene. We prayed. A feeling of uncertainty settled upon Alisa and myself.

We called back in five minutes, in ten minutes, in fifteen minutes and finally got an answer in twenty minutes. They had found Abraham after praying and frantically searching the large block which comprised our ward. Abraham had wanted to go buy something at a novelty store. (He didn't have any money and didn't even understand that he needed it to make a purchase.) He had walked a full block, crossed Springville's five-lane Main Street at dusk, then wandered up to a restaurant where our friends Johnny and Lisa Lisonbee were having dinner. They recognized him, but they didn't know the man he was talking to on the sidewalk outside the restaurant. They took him into their protective custody until our other children eventually located him there.

As a family, we acknowledged the miracle, the warning in advance that allowed all of us to pray in Abraham's behalf, and the power of family prayer in times of crisis. As a couple still driving home, the peace abounded. Tears filled our eyes as we resumed a normal speed again. We knew that the Holy Ghost had spoken to our hearts in a pure way, had protected our family in our absence while serving the Lord, and had taught our children a lesson more potent than a thousand sermons could ever have conveyed.

Sometimes our lives are so challenged that we find it overwhelming to serve others. President Gordon B. Hinckley has shared that during his full-time mission to England he wrote a letter to his father, expressing that he felt low and discouraged. His father wrote back to him in a letter:

> *Dear Gordon, I have your recent letter. I have only one suggestion: forget yourself and go to work."* [17]

President Hinckley reports that things changed for the better after he took his father's advice to *"forget yourself and go to work."*

Focusing on others first is the Lord's way for you. *"Whosoever will save his life shall lose it; but whosoever shall lose his life for my sake and the gospel's, the same shall save it."* (Mark 8:35) As Elder James E. Faust said:

> *"Recent information seems to confirm that the ultimate spiritual healing comes in the forgetting of self."* [18]

When you are low and troubled by your life's challenges, you go on about the Lord's work. While in His work and afterwards, your life's challenges fall into perspective, your mind and body are renewed by the spirit, and you feel relief from your suffering. Your calling will bring you healing and renewal through your service. You may be like Sister Fern Lisonbee who served as Relief Society President in the Spring Creek Tenth Ward while in her seventies, even after her husband died. Or like my mother, JoAnn Harris who gratefully accepted a call to visit teach the month after my step-father passed away.

The great news about the blessings which come of knowing God by serving others is that some of the most rewarding service transpires from informal service—that which happens because you feel prompted to take brownies to a neighbor, to take your friend's trash to the street, or to simply leave a kind note for someone.

Years ago, Alisa and I both had the flu. Our five small children had been complaining of hunger for over an hour. She and I had been trying to muster the energy to get up and make them something. Neither of us could get up to cook. A knock came at the door. I was lying down on the living room couch and sent our oldest son to see who was there. It was Sister Lisonbee. She had felt that she should make dinner for us. She knew I was from Georgia and prepared a large pot of chili and a pan of cornbread. We hadn't asked, but the Lord knew our needs, and Sister Lisonbee heeded the prompting of the Spirit. She responded without knowing in advance that we were sick and not knowing our children love to eat cornbread in a bowl of milk. She sat them up at the table then left without seeking even a thank you. By the way, this event occurred six years before she was called as the ward Relief Society President. We still cherish the blessing of her kindness and willingness to serve according to the Spirit's prompting.

Service to others teaches you how to be like Jesus, to follow in his ways. As the familiar Primary song goes:

"I'm trying to be like Jesus; I'm following in his ways. I'm trying to love as he did, in all that I do and say. At times I am tempted to make a wrong choice, But I try to listen as the still small voice whispers, 'Love one another as Jesus loves you. Try to show kindness in all that you do. Be gentle and loving in deed and in thought, for these are the things Jesus taught.'

I'm trying to love my neighbor; I'm learning to serve my friends. I watch for the day of gladness when Jesus will come again. I try to remember the lessons he taught. Then the Holy Spirit enters into my thoughts saying, 'Love one another as Jesus Loves You. Try to show kindness in all that you do. Be gentle and loving in deed and in thought, for these are the things Jesus taught.'" [19]

Service engulfs our troubled lives in gentle loving kindness—ours when we serve others; their's while receiving service from us; and other's while they're serving us. As Elder Joseph B. Wirthlin explained:

> *"The church is a place where imperfect people gather to provide encouragement, support, and service to each other as we press on in our journey to return to our Heavenly Father. Kindness is the essence of a celestial life. Kindness is how a Christlike person treats others. Kindness should permeate all of our words and actions at work, at school, at church, and especially in our homes."* [20]

Elder Wirthlin connects love and service through the sweet tone of kindness. Yet some of us and some whom we serve are not kind by nature. Elder Wirthlin also stated:

> *"But, you ask, 'what if people are rude?' Love them. 'If they are obnoxious?' Love them. 'But what if they offend? Surely I must do something then?' Love them. 'Wayward?' Love them. The answer is the same. Be kind. Love them. Why? In the scriptures Jude taught, 'And of some have compassion, making a difference.'"* (Jude 1:22)

All can learn kindness. And all can learn to be kind to the unkind people they serve. Elder Brockbank also said,

> *"A person who knows God would want to be like God, because God is perfect. In 1 John 4:8 we read, 'He that loveth not knoweth not God; for God is love.' As Jesus taught, 'And this is life eternal, that they might know thee the only true God, and Jesus Christ, whom thou hast sent.'"* (John 17:3)

Eternal Life → Knowing God and Jesus Christ

This means that eternal life equals intimacy with God and Jesus Christ. It equals closeness, understanding, and awareness of God and Jesus Christ. By serving those around us in kindness and love, we become like Jesus Christ, we know what He is like, we understand His ways, we become as He is. We also lose ourselves by serving others. Jesus also taught, *"If ye had known me, ye should have known my Father also: and from henceforth ye know him, and have seen Him."* *(John 14:7)*

Thus, you serve to help others. You serve to improve yourself and to change your nature into a more Christlike state which will allow you to live again in the presence of your Heavenly Father, for you will have received His image in your countenance and you will know Him because you will be like Him.

CHAPTER SIX

Learning To Love

I love you. Others love you. The Lord loves you. Who do you love? What do you love? How do you love? In the United States, love takes on a significance to relationships that is not found in many other countries throughout the world. For us, love is a prerequisite to most long-term relationships, a lost essential ingredient in the demise of most romantic relationships, and the core of interactions between family, friends, and yourself. While in many other societies, love is felt as an afterthought of relationships; love is rarely expressed verbally; and romantic love is considered folly. I like the United State's emphasis on love. I believe that here and in similar societies around the world we get needed practice in becoming like our Heavenly Father because of the abundance of love in our day-to-day lives.

Heavenly Father is loving in His nature. Jesus taught this as He prayed:

> *"Father, I will that they also, whom thou hast given me, be with me here where I am; that they may behold my glory, which thou hast given me: for thou lovedst me before the foundation of the world." (John 17:24)*

Jesus' prayer teaches you that Heavenly Father's nature is a loving nature which was with Jesus (and you) before you came to this world. Jesus wanted you to feel His Father's love, too.

"And I have declared unto them thy name, and will declare it: that the love wherewith thou hast loved me may be in them, and I in them." (John 17:26)

Heavenly Father wants you to be loving just as He is loving. In 1 John 4:8 we read, *"He that loveth not knoweth not God; for God is love."* A search of the four Standard Works reveals 554 verses that include the word "love" in one form or another. Love in the scriptures has many different usages.

Here are a few themes: to be devoted to; to sacrifice for; to serve others with; to feel connected to another person through; to receive in our hearts as a consequence of keeping commandments; to be without fear; to be loving towards others as God is loving towards us; to be charitable; to be like Jesus; to be a good neighbor, disciplinarian, or servant; and to reciprocate back to Heavenly Father His feelings towards us.

There are many other themes in the scriptures. My point is to show how God has loved men and women forever and the scriptures reflect many different types of love to help us to become loving like He is.

When I teach firesides or workshops about love, I try to emphasize that love is fluid; love changes; love is expressed many different ways; and that there is no universal way to love. I recently spoke to a friend who said she struggled just to feel love. She said that someone had expressed love to her and she knew it was sincere, but she felt nothing. I advised her not to worry. Love is there, always. Just like the sun's rays shine down even in overcast skies. Sometimes our lives are clouded by circumstances that inhibit our ability to feel love, but love is still there. Out of balance, one simple microscopic molecule of the brain's synaptic transmitters can block the feeling of love. As I encouraged my friend, I likewise encourage you to have faith that love is there.

The love of our Heavenly Father (like the rays of the sun) is always there and always in abundance. Sometimes, we feel overcast, we feel exiled to the shade, we feel buried in the world's troubles. But, His love is always there, always. It can reach down to you no matter how far you feel from it.

President Gordon B. Hinckley gave a wonderful talk in a 1989 fireside, where he shared the story of a single mother of seven children who prayed to be able to go to Heavenly Father. He said:

> "...if only for a night, to find comfort and strength for the trials of tomorrow. Tender was the response that came into her mind almost as a revelation: 'You cannot come to me, but I will come to you.'" [21]

And so it is with you, Heavenly Father's love will find you wherever you are. It will warm you, it will bring you life the same way the sun gives life to everything on the earth. There is no place too far, too dark, or too remote that exceeds our Heavenly Father's loving reach.

So, why do you (and me) often feel so far removed from Heavenly Father's love? Why do we feel so removed from the love of others? There are a few traditions, passed from generation to generation which actually inhibit your ability to love others, including Heavenly Father. I'll explain a few of these to you. But, first, I'll briefly explain how deeply love is connected to your sense of self.

It has been said that no one can love others beyond their capacity to love themselves. I'm not willing to accept that as universally true, yet I do agree with the idea that how you value yourself either opens or closes doors to how you can love others. This is why it is so important to have a true understanding of who you *really are*. To understand who you are, let's clear up a few items. The world offers a few potent distractions to knowing who your really are. It teaches that you are simply a mortal! True you were born to mortal parents, raised in a mortal family, have a mortal body, and currently live in a mortal community of friends and family. But, you did not begin at birth, nor do you end at death. You are neither the product of random natural selection, evolution, nor monkey-like ancestral heritage.

You are a child of Heavenly Parents. You have a personal Savior in Jesus Christ. You are immortal and eternal! In an April 2004 General Conference message, Neal A. Maxwell explained our true relationship to our Heavenly Father. He said:

> *"I testify to you that God has known you individually, brethren, for a long, long time. He has loved you for a long, long time. He not only knows the names of all the stars, He knows your names and all your heartaches and your joys! By the way, you never see an immortal star; they finally expire. But seated by you tonight are immortal individuals—imperfect, but who are, nevertheless, trying to be like Jesus."* [22]

To know in your soul, in every fiber of your being that you are a child of God, literally a child of God, is to allow this truth to make you free from these worldly distractions that often blind our sense of true self and misguide our efforts to love. (See John 8:32.) The plan of salvation that is taught by missionaries, taught in the Primaries, Sacrament meetings, Sunday Schools, and in the Lord's temples, is the most liberating truth about your true self. Elder Bernard P. Brockbank said:

> *"To know God, you must walk in the light of life. To know God as a living child of God, we should know our relationship to him, our divine potential."* [23]

Knowing your divine nature fills your sense of self with the love that God has for you. It allows you to love others and be loved by others with that same sweet Christlike feeling that Heavenly

Father feels for you. This is critical, because one of the first symptoms of being in love is the increase in our feelings of self. In other words, while our love grows towards the other person, so too, grows our sense of self-worth.

In general, as you interact with another person, and you accept them "as is" while they accept you "as is," your sense of self increases. As your sense of self increases, so does your ability to trust the other person. Over time, trusting leads to friendship. Friendship leads to intimacy. Increased sense of self, trust, and friendship all contribute to the love that grows between you and the other person. (See Diagram 4.)

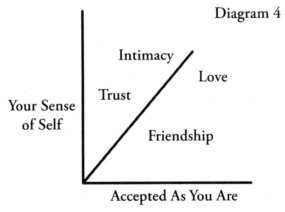

Part of love, trust, and friendship is the connection called, intimacy. Intimacy means many different things to many different people. I intend intimacy to mean a closeness that grows when you and another person open up to each other and accept each other as you both are.

Children are really good at accepting others the way they are. But, somewhere between childhood and adulthood, we become marred by the worldly view of our inadequacy and relative worthlessness. We adults tend to carry a great deal of self-shame and self-guilt with us into relationships, making it more difficult to lovingly accept who you are and then lovingly accept who others are.

Shame does not come from the Lord. Shame is adversarial and comes from sin and the influence of the adversary. Shame means a disqualification of self or another at every level. Shame assumes that you are broken, flawed, inadequate, and irreparable. Shame is a form of evil. Shame is a lie.

In Genesis 2:25 we read that Adam and Eve were both naked in the Garden of Eden *"and were not ashamed."* Shame wasn't even on the earth until the fall. The endowment teaches that the adversary shamed Adam and Eve after they had partaken of the forbidden fruit by pointing our their nakedness.

Many therapists view shame as evil and abusive to self and others. When one person disqualifies, rejects, abases, dishonors, or reproaches another, he or she has lied to the other person. Christ, himself qualified, accepted, exalted, and refined each of us through His infinite Atonement. He accepts you and invites you to come unto him, flaws and all. He heals the imperfect in you. He raises your dead or dying spirituality when you repent. He felt so strongly about you that He suffered your sins and sorrows, so that you would have another chance.

In Mosiah 14:5 we read:

> *"But he was wounded for our transgressions, he was bruised for our inequities, the chastisement of our peace was upon him; and with his stripes we are healed."*

Christ has loved you and earned the right to accept you. You, too must love and accept yourself and others in your life. To shame them is to deny the truth about their worth (your worth). To accept them is to align yourself with Christ's view of them (and of you). If doubt, criticism, and shame have plagued you (as they have me for most of my life), then consider this promise from the Savior to you which he gave while teaching the Nephites:

> *"Fear not, for thou shalt not be ashamed; neither be thou*

confounded, for thou shalt not be put to shame; for thou shalt forget the shame of thy youth, and shalt not remember the reproach of thy youth, and shalt not remember the reproach of thy widowhood anymore." (3 Nephi 22:4)

Only a witness born of the Spirit can help you to come fully unto Christ and let him remove the world's shame from your soul. Then, you can give and receive a greater measure of love. Truth be known, you are flawed (me, too). As mentioned above, you nor I can earn our way back to heaven. You cannot live perfectly then exalt yourself. You have to try your best, but it is the grace of Jesus Christ that will ultimately make up the difference and yield you worthy to stand in Heavenly Father's presence once more.

Accepting yourself and your flaws with a steadfast hope that Christ will make up the difference in the final judgement is humbling. It's also a deeply healing truth. You are flawed and I love you. You are flawed and Heavenly Father loves you. Christ loves you "as is." He accepts your efforts to repent. Don't interfere with His divine Atonement by self-shaming or other-shaming. Also avoid self-guilt.

Guilt is often a distraction. If it helps you to avoid sin and to be a better friend or family member then so let it be. Yet, many of us afflict our selves with needless guilt. This statement implies that there is a needed guilt. Perhaps, when we do commit a sin, guilt can motivate us to repent, to change, to come back to Heavenly Father. But, guilt is a terrible motivation for change, even when the change is good for us. Studies have shown that guilt only compounds efforts to break addictions. It rarely if ever, leads people to avoid repeating behaviors that are unwanted pleasures.

What does work then, if guilt doesn't? The simple truth is that love motivates us to change 1,000 times more than guilt ever could. Love for those we sometimes hurt, love for ourselves, and love for our Savior and Heavenly Father.

I personally know people who have found the strength to give up addictions, have been able to become full-tithe payers, and have broken the cyclic chain of hurting family and friends because they feel love for Heavenly Father which spilled over to love for themselves. They were willing to turn to the Lord and change. When people realize that their actions hurt themselves, others, and ultimately Heavenly Father, they, out of sheer love for Him, pray for and find the ability to change. Change does and really should come slowly and prayerfully. Have you ever dieted and lost lots of pounds in a week or two, only to regain it in a week or two? I have. Diets work best which take place over a period of time with gradual loss of weight. Slow, steady changes "line upon line," as the scripture says:

> *"For he will give unto the faithful line upon line, precept upon precept; and I will try you and prove you herewith."* (D&C 98:12)

Change is like that. It's effective piece by piece over time. When you try to change you should choose one specific behavior to change (such as to express your love to a family member every day). Then you should let yourself change through three distinct stages. First, you catch yourself in the old behavior after the fact (say you notice that you've ended the day without having verbally expressed your feelings of love to a family member).

Second, you catch yourself in the act of the old behavior (you nearly hang up the phone when you realize you forgot to express your love).

Third, you begin to see the circumstances that contribute to repeating the old behavior and forgetting the new desired behavior (you come to realize that at the end of long days at work you become more forgetful). In the third stage you're approaching a sustainable and enduring change and you come to recognize that certain factors inhibit while others promote the changed behavior. You manage them accordingly (you call midday to say you love your sister, anticipating the effect of the hard day on your memory).

In review of the three stages of change, the first stage is when you repeat unwanted behavior and only recognize it after the fact. The second stage is when you catch yourself repeating unwanted behaviors while in the act of doing them. And third you begin to recognize patterns that contribute to your repeating unwanted behaviors—you see the behaviors coming.

Expressing your love to others is good practice for expressing your love to and receiving love from your Heavenly Father. There are different ways to express love. You can say it, verbally. You can show it in actions and service. You can touch, hug, pamper, caress, hold, and kiss. You can sacrifice time, talents, and resources for others. You can give when nothing is offered in response to your gift. You can receive their expressions of love toward you.

Love is risky for many people. But, you can learn to safely navigate love as you learn to incorporate Heavenly Father's love into your own. Love is much more like a river than a lake. Rivers have a destination. Rivers constantly travel and encounter new terrain around each bend. Rivers provide life to regions surrounding them. Rivers must be respected more than lakes (lakes tend to be safer). Rivers overcome obstacles or simply cut a new path around them.

In 2001, Alisa and I went on a business trip to Jackson County, Missouri. While there we attended an exhibit about an excavated steamboat called the Steamboat Arabia. It was built in 1853, was flat and wide like many boats of its day. And it sank with a full load of cargo after it hit a tree snag in the water. After it sank, the silt and debris of the river buried it. In 1980 a team of locals dug it up.

Because it had been buried in deep, cold silt, the excavators found bottled fruits and pickles (which they ate and enjoyed twelve decades after it sank in the Missouri River). Interestingly, the shipwreck was found hundreds of yards from the river's current path. The river had, over time, cut new banks, washed away old banks, and changed its course repeatedly.

If rivers are like love then loving is a great deal like riding a raft down the river. Rivers can be gentle, slow moving, and calm at times. But, some rivers are fast, treacherous, dangerous, and potentially deadly at other times. In fact there's an organization in the U.S. that classifies rivers and their rapids. (Look up Americanwhitewater.org on the Internet.) They rate rapids between 1 and 6. (1=easy; 2=novice; 3=intermediate; 4=advanced; 5=expert; and 6=extreme.) I studied their rating system and identified the criteria they use to assign classes to rapids. Consider these criteria as they might also be applied to loving.

The criteria are: they consider how easy it is to avoid a rapid if you want to do so; how predictable the ride through the rapids might be for an average person; the risk of danger in a specific section of the river; types of obstruction near the rapid; and the likelihood of rescue if a crisis occurs.

We can apply the same criteria to the risks associated with taking risks in a loving relationship: you consider how easy it is to avoid the loving relationship if you want to do so; how predictable the ride through the risks of the loving relationship might be for an average person; the risk of danger in a specific section of the loving relationship (say before the DTR=Defining The Relationship encounter); types of obstruction near the loving relationship; and the likelihood of rescue if a crisis of trust occurs to the loving relationship.

Don't get the wrong idea. You do not need to become Class 6 experts at loving relationships. You simply need to turn prayerfully to the Lord so that He can help us love as you are called upon to love. You can and should learn how to know your divine nature and incorporate that into your sense of self; into learning to avoid self-shame and self-guilt; and into loving others as Jesus Christ and Heavenly Father love you. You can and must let the Atonement heal you, daily so that you can trust and be trusted, build and give friendship, and let the confidence of the Lord guide your process of loving growth and change.

Doesn't the following song remind you of how the Savior loves us, and wants us all to love?

"As I have loved you, love one another. This new commandment: Love one another. By this shall men know, ye are my disciples, if ye have love one to another." [24]

CHAPTER SEVEN

Drawing the Line for Healthy Boundaries

For decades professional therapists have been improving the lives of their patients by teaching them skills in maintaining boundaries. The main reason that boundary maintenance is so critical to recovery is that weak boundaries are such a common side effect and symptom of so many relationship disorders. To maintain them is to restore order and to prevent many future entanglements between people.

Nature uses boundaries everywhere. Your body is comprised of billions of cells. Each has its own membrane that distinguishes it from other cells. Your skin surrounds your body and it sets a boundary around you—one that must be respected according to your rules. Your clothes, your car, and your home are all extensions of your body that distinguish your uniqueness to others. They too must be respected according to your rules.

You essentially become the director of boundaries in your life. You decide if you'll let another drive your car and you loan the car keys accordingly. You decide who will visit you in your home and you open the door to let them in when they arrive and out when it's time for them to leave. You have a God-given right and responsibility to become skilled at understanding boundaries and using them wisely.

You also have God-given direction on how to do this. Commandments, teachings, and inspired instruction from church leaders provide boundaries set by the Lord to help you succeed. Following them is an act of obedience. It's also an act of wisdom to heed the voice of the Lord who has the skills and knowhow to help you become exalted.

The Lord has boundaries, too. In the temple, the Lord's house, only those who qualify can enter and be in the near-presence of our Heavenly Father. According to the Lord's boundaries, you have to be recommended by our bishop and stake president. Other boundaries include the fact that: only a bishop can approve Aaronic Priesthood ordinances in the ward; inspiration follows a line of authority; the Lord respects agency in you; and only the prophet has the right to revelation for the entire church.

I want to teach you a simple metaphor that will help you to understand and maintain your boundaries from this time on and throughout the rest of your life. I call the metaphor "My House, My Boundaries." In your real life, you put locks and latches on your real house doors and windows to keep intruders out. This paradigm will teach you how to put healthy relationship locks and latches in your interpersonal relationships, so that only those you choose to invite into your house will be allowed in and at a level of interaction that you are comfortable with. Diagram 5 shows the basic floor-plan of a house and yard.

Each of you has a boundary like an

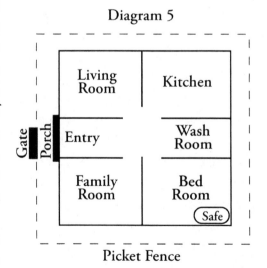

Diagram 5

invisible house. It exists at many levels—spiritual, physical, intellectual, emotional, and social. Your invisible house represents these diverse types of boundaries. Think of yourself as having a personal house which exists in the suburbs of your many interpersonal relationships.

As mentioned, you have the responsibility of taking charge of your own house. That means you choose which people you invite in, when they are invited in, and which level of closeness in your house you'll allow them to share with you. You also have the responsibility of ensuring that you don't violate others' house boundaries. On the floor plan included above, think of the house in terms of varying levels of intimate or personal interaction with others. The fence is the most superficial level of interaction; whereas the bedroom is the deepest level.

The Picket Fence represents our outer edge, our ability to associate with strangers at stores, banks, and in other public settings. I choose a picket fence because we all need some transparency to let others see that we are normal, safe, and much like everyone else. I often joke that some who've been hurt choose a different type fence than the picket fence. They choose a 10-foot concrete wall with razor wire mounted on the wall and with machine guns posted on every corner, threatening anyone who dares to try to get close. This is not a sound way to make friends. Still, others have no fence, no doors, and no windows in their house (another bad idea).

Let's consider the other sections of this house and their meanings as a metaphor for levels of intimacy, using the example of you moving into a new ward. The Gate is where you typically interact with people you don't yet know. You say "hello, hi, how's it goin?" We often don't really want to have the person respond. These are simply polite greetings we use with people we don't know.

The Porch & Entry Way is for people you are getting to

know better, say another person you sit next to in Sunday School (both you and they wait on the porch, hoping to be invited into the other's house). You invite them into your house when you introduce yourself to them.

"Hello. I'm Sister McGee. Who are you?" you might ask.

"I'm Sister Gonzales," she replies. "Are you new to the ward?"

"Yes. This is my first Sunday here," you answer. "How about you? Have you been in this ward long?"

Once superficial details are shared, you've both symbolically entered the house into the Entry Way. The sharing of personal information about: your name, where you are from, or your job is common when initiating intimacy with a stranger. At these levels you rarely share extremely personal information. That is reserved for people you have known for a long time and already trust.

Let's say that after a few weeks in this ward, and after sitting next to the same sister each Sunday, you get invited to watch a video. Once in her home, you find yourselves sharing deeper personal information that requires a greater measure of trust on both parts.

"Have a seat on the sofa," Sister Gonzales might say, sitting in the chair next to you. "So, tell me about yourself. Where are you from?" she continues. You answer and repeat the same type of questions back to her. These might include information about your family, career aspirations, history as a member of the church, and the like. Sister Gonzales brings in some snacks and you watch the video together. You are now interacting at the Living Room level in your house. You share information but are still guarded about the more vulnerable things about yourself.

After months (sometimes years) of interacting safely, you may feel safe enough to establish a deeper friendship by asking more intimate questions and likewise sharing more intimate details about yourself. In the Kitchen you tend to share more personal information, especially after more than one visit and after the friendship deepens. In this level of interacting, you have deeply established trust and can share your fears, concerns, weaknesses, struggles, relationship challenges, and hopes with someone in conversation. In the kitchen, confidences are kept. Each knows and respects this fact. The kitchen is often the deepest level of intimacy between friends.

"So, tell me the real reason you moved from a family ward to a singles ward?" You might ask. If Sister Gonzales answers truthfully, you'd probably be expected to answer the same question back to her. That's the key to understanding intimacy—it has to be reciprocated at about the same level of risks. If Sister Gonzales answered your question, but you would not tell her why you joined the singles ward, trust would feel violated.

The Family Room represents a somewhat unique level of interacting that is appropriate to the family but not necessarily to others outside of the family system. Family jokes, stories, traditions, embarrassing moments, and other appropriate interactions are shared in this room.

The Bedroom represents the deepest level of intimacy that you can experience. This is not only where you sleep, change clothes and pray, it's a haven from the rest of the house and the rest of society. It represents the level you know yourself at, the level the Lord knows you at, and the level very few others ever get to know you at. Here you express intimacy at the most intimate level. You can think of the bedroom as representing a sanctuary where even the closest companions are not welcomed. Here, under protected circumstances social, spiritual, and emotional intimacy can flourish.

In the bedroom you are seen by the Lord as Adam and Eve were seen before their fall. Adam and Eve were seen physically naked. But, you are seen at the level of your naked soul. This implies that you are your "true naked self" here—no defenses, pretensions, walls, or mask are found. In other words, your Savior hears and answers your prayers, knowing your less apparent flaws and strengths. Jesus hears your cellular honesty and your soul's desires. He knows your true heart, and continually invites you to come unto Him, even though He also is fully aware of your imperfections. That's what I love about Jesus. He looks into the depth of my soul, sees my scars, wounds, peculiarities and loves me still the same.

In your bedroom, you have a Safe. Your safe represents the most intimate, vulnerable, and personal part of who you are and how you feel about yourself. You rarely open it, even in prayer. But, the Lord knows all and knows (and respects) what you guard within it. When you do open your safe, you must do so with the utmost self-respect and dignity. This takes practice, time, and lots of patient self-forgiveness.

Only you know the combination to your safe and you choose when to open and close it. Prayer is the safest time to open your safe. Imagine your Savior listening to you while you both sit under a shade tree in the cool of the evening. Imagine His unwavering devotion and ask Him to help you to express what is deep in your heart. Imagine His perfect recall of the accomplishments you've made, the times when He and you conquered a challenge together, and the encouragement only He could give to your fondest dreams. Now open up to Him. If doubts arise, they come from within you. Ask Him to help you work through them He will. Part of knowing God is to let Him know you.

Boundaries in general can be learned with practice. But, you'd be well prepared to anticipate that others won't be much help in maintaining them. For example, the challenge of removing extended family members from the bedroom level (especially intruding parents) becomes a burden if the problem goes ignored. I have heard horror stories of parents interfering with their adult children's relationship by: giving unsolicited financial, relationship, and intimate advice; setting up financial deals which keep the children indebted to them; forcing "the way they did things" as the right way upon their adult child; and over-involving their adult children in their extended family so that their children have to struggle to establish their own family traditions and customs.

Adult children sometimes have to be extremely diligent in removing parents or other family and friend offenders from their bedroom-level issues. If this is the case for you, then keep in mind that in the long run, it will be worth it. Relationships tend to be healthier and people tend to be happier when these house-like boundaries are maintained. Many encounter resistance to establishing healthy boundaries in family systems that had few. Be patient and persistent.

The other room represents another unique concept in this paradigm. The Washroom represents a place where you can clean up the messes people sometimes bring into your house. For example, sometimes others get too personal with you and can be offensive at times. I call this a home invasion. Home invasion questions sound like this, "You know what you've been doing wrong in raising these kids? Don't you see the huge financial error in how you're saving your money?" Some even ask extremely intimate questions without regard to propriety.

It's like some people trudge around in the pig sty of their own human relationships, then trample your floor with their soiled boots(often by asking unwanted questions or sharing unsolicited personal information). You have to remove them from within your house to beyond the porch or gate.

There are a few key guidelines in removing people to a more appropriate level of intimacy when this happens: 1, simply distract the other person with a change in subject; 2, don't laugh at their jokes or give them approval, even if you're feeling nervous (boundary violators tend to be approval addicts who push limits to the max); 3, gently confront the violation while teaching them why it feels like a violation to you (*"How I parent my children is my own business and your unsolicited advice shows little respect for me as an individual"* or *"Have you ever thought about why I might not feel comfortable hearing your unintended parenting advice?"*); 4, express your frustration in having them violate your boundaries (*"I appreciate that you helped me to move into my new apartment, Dad, but I feel so frustrated that you give me unsolicited parenting advice that I did not ask for"*); and/or 5, confront boundary violators somewhat sternly and if need be, discontinue the relationship if the boundary violations persist (*"I just can't spend more time with you because your boundary violations are too troublesome for me to deal with"*). Ignorance on their part is not an excuse for continued violations.

After you remove them to the level of interacting you are comfortable with, you can symbolically wash their muddy footprints out of your rug, forgive, and get on with other things. As was mentioned before, you are responsible for maintaining the level of interaction in your house. Practice by following the commandments/boundaries the Lord has set for you. Practice by interacting at levels that you define as comfortable and appropriate for you. Many in our society are conditioned <u>not</u> to respect boundaries and most who don't are not even aware of why it is such an unhealthy practice.

You should also be aware that the opposite of a home invasion can also occur. This is called a boundary kidnaping—where you are dragged into the intimate personal lives of others without warning or permission (i.e.: *I need to tell you about my ex-spouse's secrets*). The same strategies given for managing invasions also work for managing kidnappings.

I've taught a number of singles firesides and conferences where I've encouraged singles to state "what" their status is, but not "why" their status is the way it is (i.e.: *I'm single, divorced and the father of two, but not why things are that way*). The details of "why" often include the spreading of poisonous gossip, the violation of confidences, and the often unintended violation of boundaries (both yours and the person listening to you). Ultimately the details of the "why" are a violation and re-offense of yourself more than the other person.

I have compared the details of relationships gone sour to a "barrel of toxic waste." Close the toxic barrel, hammer the lid shut, bury it with your feelings of hurt as you heal and recover. Only you can reopen the barrel. That holds true even if you are asked very personal questions.

You can choose not to answer any questions that trudge up the old poisons of relationships long ended. If you open the barrel, by sharing details of what happened, you risk opening healed wounds again.

Yes details can and should be shared in the right place, at the right time, and with the right individual. "Whys" can be discussed with caution, but that typically occurs in established, long-term, and trusting relationships and not on the dance floor with a new acquaintence.

I once gave a talk in St. George, Utah. After I finished my talk a woman came up to me and said that she disagreed with my toxic barrel metaphor.

"Why?" I asked.

"I'm dating a man who has been divorced seven times. I need to know what happened so I can know what I'm getting into," she explained.

"Oh," I replied. "What's he like?"

"He's nice enough, but I'm not really sure yet what he's like. We've only been out twice so far."

"Then here's my challenge to you," I said. "As you date, find out what he's like now—his character, his love of the Lord, his desire to serve, his respect of the opposite sex . . . you know, things that really matter."

"I don't know," she said. "I still feel the need to hear why those seven marriages ended."

"Do you think that a man who has been divorced seven times will or even can tell you exactly why those marriages ended?" I asked. "Do you think he'll be honest about it?"

That was about the end of the conversation. We shook hands and parted on friendly terms. She still disagreed with my toxic waste barrel metaphor. I was okay with that. She's sharp enough to discern truth from error and I'm sure my point was taken. But she opened my eyes to the intense risks of establishing relationships. "The stakes are extremely high and the market is brutal," a person at a Utah Valley conference said to me.

I agree, with the emphasis that high stakes and brutal markets do not exceed the Lord's Atonement and healing power and that maintaining boundaries will only increase your ability to navigate through them. Maintaining boundaries is also, in a small way, an act of gratitude towards the Savior for the healing you've already experienced with Him. Jesus said:

> *"For it is not meet that the things which belong to children of the kingdom should be given to them that are not worthy, or to dogs, or the pearls to be cast before swine." (D&C 41:6)*

This is very strong language (dogs and swine). In the verse's footnote, the Topical Guide reference refers to pearls as "holiness." We're talking here about proper boundaries of information and stories too sacred to share with just anyone. Average things belong in average conversations. Sacred things belong in sacred conversations. Intimacies and confidence, if respected and protected help to maintain healthy boundaries.

You are the very best judge of specifically what is sacred, average and confidential. You are the best resource for establishing your own healthy boundaries. Keep in mind that this paradigm is based on the belief that personal boundary maintenance is really about interacting with others appropriately, based on your true feelings, needs, and wants. It is not about controlling others. It is about self-control and to a large degree honesty with your self. It's also about self-protection. As a dear friend said, "If you don't have boundaries, you can be everything to others while being nothing to yourself."

CHAPTER EIGHT

Choose Happiness

"Don't Worry. Be Happy." These simple words sang by Bobby McFerrin in 1988 topped the *Billboard Magazine* charts in nearly every country in the world and also won numerous awards. What a simple concept with such a powerful message! The words of the song advise the listener to let the bad things pass by and be happy in spite of them. You might be thinking, "It sounds simple, but not always so easy to pull off."

My Granddaddy Oliver would always say, "I'm such a worrier, that if every thing is going well, I'll start worrying about what's about to go wrong." Worry may even have genetic origins. The fact is, my mother, my siblings, and I struggle with patterns of worry. Worrying also is a learned human behavior. The same can be said of happiness (genetic and learned). Are you like me, genetically predisposed to worry while rarely feeling happiness? If so, there's good news—any genetic predisposition can be overcome through diligent effort, obedience to commandments, and faith in the Lord.

I come from a long line of addicts. Alcohol, tobacco, substances, TV viewing, eating, and even shopping plague both sides of my family. It's definitely in the family culture. One of the best things my wife and I ever did was to study the LDS version of the 12 Steps Program. We took it because we needed help coping with family members' addictions. You see, obeying the Word of Wisdom spared both of us from having serious addictive experiences. We still suffer from the disobedience of our family and friends.

As far as happiness goes, my wife is one of the happiest people I've ever known. But, she married me, the guy who's mission president had to assign someone to help me learn to be happy. In the 20 years we've been married, I've learned to feel more happiness. I'll never forget Bishop Parker at Ricks College (1985-1986) who taught us that either you have money or you don't. It really doesn't matter, because it's up to us to decide at the end of the month to be happy, regardless of where the budget ends up (in the red or in the black).

That was the first realization I had that happiness comes from within me and results from my attitude not my circumstances. I made up a little acronym for the word, HAPPY to help me remember strategies for feeling happy. It goes like this:

Honk just when the cat jumps onto the hood of your car when you've pulled into the driveway.

Act like you just won $60,000 from the *Jeopardy* game show the next time the 7-11 clerk gives you back your change.

Pretend to fall asleep in a fireside then jolt up to your feet when the person next to you gives you a nudge (I bet he or she will have a hard time keeping a straight face).

Pretend the applause is for you and take a bow at the end of the next concert you attend.

Yodel the Smiles song, "If you chance to meet a frown..." while driving alone.

Okay, okay. Admittedly, these are laugh-producing activities that should be employed only for carefully selected moments. Laughing is great medicine for feeling happy. I found hundreds of Internet references that teach people why and how laughter heals the body and soul. You see, laughing lowers blood pressure, releases positive endorphins, increases oxygen content in the blood, shifts attitudes upward, lowers feelings of depression, relieves stress and anxiety, and contagiously influences others in positive ways. (See thisisawar.com; indiadiets.com; thinkquest. org's laugh out loud; AMA-assn.org; thelouisvillechannel.com; ivanhoe.com or search laughter and health in your Webpage for links to numerous resources.)

Norman Cousins wrote a book titled *Anatomy of An Illness.* In the 1980s it proved to be a bestseller and a groundbreaking work about using humor among other things to beat back serious illness.

One of the best and recent examples of laughter in the LDS Church is with President Gordon B. Hinckley. He loves to laugh and to joke so others may also laugh. I've heard him speak in person and found myself laughing, pondering, and praying all in the same talk. President Hinckley has given us permission to be happy, to laugh, and to find joy in what we do. There's wisdom in following his example. I also have a principle-based acronym for the word, HAPPY that leads to feeling happiness. It's presented in more of a serious tone.

> **H** is for honoring all my covenants each and every day (wickedness never was happiness).
>
> **A** is for adapting my lifestyle to include happiness and happiness-supporting behaviors.
>
> **P** is for praying for enough faith to be happy in the presence of unwanted and unchangeable circumstances that I willingly turn over to the Lord to manage.
>
> **P** is for practicing gratitude . . . "count your many blessings, name them on by one."
>
> **Y** is for yearning in your soul to happily enjoy life each and every day, forever.

In a talk by Elder Robert D. Hales in 1995, he taught that our Heavenly Father wants and has always wanted happiness for you in your life. He said:

"Because of his great love for each of us, the Lord wants all of us to be happy. He has told us through the prophet Lehi, 'Men are, that they might have joy." (2 Nephi 2:25) This joy we speak of is in the present. We do not have to wait for another day, another year, until our circumstances change, or until we pass through the veil and go to our celestial glory. We are to find joy in the present. If we love the gospel of Jesus Christ, we can find joy in whatever condition we find ourselves." [25]

The Lord wants you to be happy today, tomorrow, and each day for the rest of your life. I want you to come to know that it is up to *you* to choose happiness. No one else can choose your happiness. Attitudes are controlled from within. You and only you can choose to take on the role of adventurer for the Lord as you "boldly go" where you've never been before.

Imagine that one day you catch a bad cold. You ache all over. You can't breathe through your nose. Your throat is too sore to swallow. You just feel like staying in bed. Instead you decide to force yourself to drive to the drug store. There you are, standing in the cold-remedy section. You have thirty different varieties of cold-relief medicines to choose from. Some are natural some are pharmaceutical. One makes you sleepy and drowsy to the point that you can't even function in your daily tasks while on them. Others cause no drowsiness and treat one, two, and as many as seven different symptoms of the common cold. Which do you choose? If you're like me and most others, you're looking for relief from your specific symptoms of aches and pains.

So you study each label trying to find the best relief while spending the least amount of money. Any of the products would offer some relief. What if you studied all the products for an hour then walked away, refusing to buy any of them? That might sound absurd. But, many people do this, when it comes to choosing happiness. They have many outlets and opportunities to choose activities that bring relief from unhappiness. They study them. Yet they choose not to pursue them. Some choose to simply stay in bed and suffer, figuratively speaking. Why? Because, they are waiting for the symptoms to leave before they'll seek relief rather than choosing to be happy now, with or without the symptoms.

The time to choose happiness is right now. Now, the present is all we have. The past cannot be changed. The future cannot be predicted. The now is when you get out of the bed of your unhappiness and search out and choose happiness. Remember what Paul said in his epistle to the Philippians:

> *"Not that I speak in respect of want: for I have learned, in whatsoever state I am, therewith to be content." (Philippians 4:11)*

Your choice is simple. Choose happiness in the state you are currently in. You can't wait for parenting, relationships, work, success, finances, callings, friendships, status, and health to improve before you become happy. You must choose relief while you need it.

I began this book on my vacation time. It was limited and I knew I had to work diligently to stay on schedule. Late one Saturday evening, I was teaching our two youngest sons, Abraham and Isaac (yes, their older brother, next in line, is named Jacob) how to disassemble a computer hard drive. They were too young to be fully employed, so I wanted them to recycle computers to make a little money. As I pulled the steel lid from the aluminum hard drive case, I sliced both my pointer and middle fingers on my right hand. I received a total of five stitches.

The cut and stitches were not too serious except that I was

typing this book at the time. You see, I never learned how to type. I tried, but, some things are difficult for me and typing is one of them. I hunt and peck with the pointer fingers on my left and right hands. The timing and inspiration came for this book during the same ten day period the stitches had to remain in my fingers. So, I kept hunting and pecking at the keys, using my ring finger of the right hand. Try this at home, typing with your ring finger of your dominant hand.

My story is admittedly trivial in many ways. I could have talked about our friend who tours the country each summer with one of her friends. I could have talked about another friend who took up running marathons after her 56th birthday. I also could have talked about another friend who earned his college degree, while raising his three children and working full-time. All of these case studies illustrate the same point—that now is the time to live, to do, and to be happy (stitches or no stitches, wealth or no wealth, status or no status, health or no health).

There are many guidelines given by the Lord through His prophets and apostles (cold remedies on the shelf if you will). We don't have to invent the remedy, we simply choose the one that best fits our needs for symptom relief. Let me mention a key issue. It has been pointed out to me that cold remedies do not cure the cold, only relieve the symptoms. Happiness, like cold remedies, does not cure the challenges we face. It's just the best known way to relieve the negative symptoms that result from our tribulations—depression, fatigue, grief, and sorrow.

One of the most effective ways to choose happiness is to express gratitude to the Lord in our prayers. We all have been taught to begin prayers by addressing our Heavenly Father, expressing our gratitude for our blessings, asking for those things we stand in need, then closing the prayer in the name of Jesus Christ. Thankfulness and gratitude are important to our Heavenly Father. He asks us to express our thankfulness before we request the blessings we stand in need of. Not expressing gratitude is offensive to your Heavenly Father. The Lord said:

> *"And in nothing doth man offend God, or against none is His wrath kindled, save those who confess not His hand in all things, and obey not His commandments." (D&C 59:21)*

Expressing gratitude to your Heavenly Father actually brings blessings, including prosperity. The Lord said:

> *"And who receiveth all things with thankfulness shall be made glorious; and the things of this earth shall be added unto him, even a hundred fold, yea more." (D&C 78:19)*

Moroni gives readers of the Book of Mormon a promise, that if they read it, ask God with a sincere heart about it, having faith in Christ, then Christ will manifest the truth of the Book of Mormon to them. Notice in Moroni 10:3 how Moroni recommends that readers take note of the mercies of God unto men. He urges readers to have a thankful attitude toward God.

> *"Behold, I would exhort you that when ye shall read these things, if it be wisdom in God that ye should read them, that ye would remember how merciful the Lord hath been unto the children of men."*

Moroni *then* gives the promise of gaining a witness. Gratitude precedes the receipt of more blessings. I want you to try an experiment for one month. In your personal prayers, give thanks ten times for every one blessing you ask for. Sometimes it becomes difficult to think of what you're thankful for. With practice, gratitude to the Lord becomes more and more easy to feel.

Thank the Lord for family, friends, children's laughter, nature's beauty, financial blessings, health, pitfalls that were avoided, service you gave and received, righteous outcomes in the lives of people you care about, assistance received from the Lord during the day, safety, food, basic needs being met, your life, the tribulations you do not have to endure, covenants, church and your personal church membership, the temple, home and visiting teachers, callings, the Sacrament, lessons taught, moments of having felt the Holy Spirit's influence, your afflictions, enduring through hardship, forgiveness, the gospel, Joseph Smith, living prophets and apostles, stake presidency, bishopric, transportation, your Savior's Atonement and personal love for you, Heavenly Parents, the great plan of salvation, the little things that gave you strength throughout the day, etc.

I think you can start with some of these and add those things you're grateful for. The more you express gratitude the more you feel gratitude.

Elder Richard C. Edgley, First Counselor in the Presiding Bishopric, gave a talk about how humility empowers members throughout the world. He connected gratitude and humility as "twin characteristics" when he said:

> *"As I have pondered these faithful members, I am struck by two qualities they all seem to have. First, regardless of social or economic status or position, their humility leads to submissiveness to the Lord's will. And second, in spite of the difficulties and trials of life, they are able to maintain a sense of gratitude for God's blessings and life's goodness. Humility and gratitude are truly the twin characteristics of happiness"* [26]

Elder Edgley pointed out that gratitude makes us better people, more submissive and humble. This is in part why the Lord expects gratitude from us. More gratitude makes us more like Him. Yes, more gratitude within you will bring about more happiness within you.

I have a dear friend. Her name is Ingrid Perkins. She and her family joined the church in Germany before World War II. Her father was investigated and arrested by the Nazis more than once while serving as branch president during the war. After the war, she served a full-time mission then migrated to Utah. She married Harold Perkins. They had only one daughter. Ingrid worked many years then retired as a nurse. She is by far one of the happiest people I know.

Ingrid is not wealthy. Ingrid is not famous. Ingrid is simply happy. Upon her refrigerator door she has one phrase, *"Happiness is A Conscious Choice."* This has always struck me, because Ingrid has been through a great deal of affliction. She survived: World War II, poverty, hunger, and lean times. She also survived: nearly a decade of caring for her Alzheimer-stricken husband before he died; the loss of her young adult daughter to cancer; the death of many close relatives; and the passage of decades as the only person living in her home. Why is Ingrid Perkins so happy?

Ingrid makes the conscious choice to be happy. She schedules her time to include healthy occupations. She has worked for nearly a decade as a teacher's assistant in the local elementary school. By the way, she was awarded an Outstanding Educator award by the Jon and Karen Huntsman Foundation. She serves in her ward callings. She exercises daily, including maintenance of her home, yard, and garden. She has many friends and social gatherings. Though her health is declining she continues to choose happiness and spreads it to others in her life. On my fortieth birthday she told me with a sly grin, *"Ron, you are forty years old and now old enough to be considered mature."* I love Ingrid and she loves me.

What Ingrid and many others already know is that choosing happiness includes choosing things that support happiness while you're in need of them. Keeping busy for yourself and others is healthy. Most theories about successful aging center around how happy older persons stay connected and involved. It's true for old and young alike.

The ward is a wonderful organization to facilitate that connectedness and involvement. Elder Robert D. Hales said:

"We all belong to a community of saints, we all need each other, and we are all working toward the same goal. Any one of us could isolate ourselves from this ward family on the basis of our differences. But we must not shut ourselves out or isolate ourselves from opportunities because of the differences we perceive in ourselves. Instead, let us share our gifts and talents with others, bringing brightness of hope and joy to them, and in so doing lift our own spirits." [27]

Give yourself to the membership of the ward family. Let your happiness improve the collective feeling of love in your ward. Don't wait until the ward changes for you. You change your ward and ward members with your service. They need your help, love, and service.

Elder James E. Faust quoted President Spencer W. Kimball as saying:

"Happiness does not depend upon what happens outside of you, but on what happens inside of you. It is measured by the spirit with which you meet the problems of life." [28]

Once you choose to be happy, you can influence others around you in your hidden and open acts of service, especially to the members of your own ward family. Elder John K. Carmack taught:

"Look up from your life, and look outward to what you can do to contribute. Strive for balance in your life, and blessings you need will be added to you. Balance includes friendship and love for family and associates, goals and directions, stability and control, good external support systems (family, friends, and church leaders), obedience to gospel standards, maintenance of high morale, and substantial outward contributions to others." [29]

Elder Carmack warned to avoid constantly thinking about ourselves about how we feel and look outward. Self-concern is diminished as other-concern and other-service is increased. President Gordon B. Hinckley also taught us to look beyond ourselves:

> *"You are a child of God, His crowning creation. After He had formed the earth, separated the darkness from the light, divided the waters, created the plant and animal kingdoms——after all this He created man and then woman. I repeat, I hope you will never demean or belittle yourselves. Some of you may think you are not attractive, that you have no talents. Stop wandering around in the wasteland of self-pity. The greatest missionary the world has known, the Apostle Paul, is said to have been short, have a large Roman nose, rounded shoulders, and a whining voice, all of which may not sound too attractive to some persons. Abraham Lincoln, America's greatest hero, was tragically homely. But from his great heart and mind came words such as few other men have spoken."* [30]

The best way to forget about you is to do something for someone else. I want you to try another experiment for one month. Pick a ward member. Find some way to secretly serve that person during the week. It doesn't have to be anything major. Small service often means more than larger acts of service. Next week, pick another person.

Do the same thing four consecutive weeks in a row. Take notice of ward conversations and individual behaviors. Discreetly study the impact you made in these persons' lives. Now repeat this assignment again. Be grateful for the opportunity to serve others.

What should be your disposition while serving your ward members? The Lord said about fasting and prayer:

"And inasmuch as ye do these things with thanksgiving, with cheerful hearts and countenances, not with much laughter, for this is a sin, but with a glad heart and a cheerful countenance." (D&C 59:15)

Cheerful hearts and countenances work for fasting and for happiness while serving others. But, if cheerful isn't something you do easily, this scripture may sound like an impossibility to you. It did for me for many years. In fact, my second missionary companion, serving with me in Grenoble, France, informed me that his top assignment from the mission president was to teach me how to enjoy life and be happy while serving the Lord. Robert Walker was the best guy to teach me how to be happy and I'm much happier now because of his influence on me. I'm happy to say he succeeded. I still repeat some of his antics with my own children today and they love it!

Some of us struggle physiologically to be happy. I love this scripture in the second epistle of Paul to Timothy:

"For God hath not given us the spirit of fear; but of power, and of love, and of a sound mind." (2 Timothy 1:7)

Here's the third experiment—pray daily for your fears to be cast off through the Atonement of Jesus Christ. Pray also for power, love, and a sound mind. The Lord will award this to you as He sees fit. I urge you to pray for people to come into your life who can serve as a role model for happiness. They can't make you happy, only you can do that. But, they can set an example of how they find happiness and you can learn from them.

Remember that happiness is not so much a destination (like on *Gilligan's Island*) it's much more like a never ending voyage (like on *Star Trek*). Make a choice now to get up off your unhappy sick bed and pursue your remedies for happiness. Over time, you will gain more and more confidence as a happy person and happiness will become second nature to you.

I hope there has been a nugget or two of valuable information to help you have a quality journey in your life. My closing prayer for you is that the challenges of your journey don't distract so much that you feel separated from the Lord's love. I pray that you allow the Lord to be a part of your mortality; to help heal you especially when you feel isolated in your mortal travels.

I pray that you invite the Lord to sustain you in your quest to know God, to know who you really are; to endure, to choose faith and happiness, to call upon the grace and healing of your Savior Jesus Christ as you learn to trust again; to serve others; to love as God loves; to keep healthy boundaries; and to become as we all desire to be—sons and daughters of a Heavenly Father with whom we live for eternity.

Post Script

————— ✦ —————

Where you stand right now,
at this very moment, come unto Christ.
If you can't stand it's where you sit or lie.
But, now, this very breath, come unto Christ.
Draw upon His love like you would draw upon a
Swiss bank account that has an eternal supply of
healing, bonding, strengthening,
and recovering resources at your disposal.
The journey is often perilous.
Christ freely gives us these spiritual travelers checks.
So, ask for them often and spend them regularly
throughout your spiritual journey because,
it's all about the journey.

Endnotes

1. Maxwell, Neal A. "Insights from My Life," *Ensign,* Aug. 2000, p. 7.

2. Maxwell, Neal A. "Swallowed Up in the Will of the Father," *Ensign,* Nov. 1995, p. 22.

3. Burton, Theodore M. "Salvation for the Dead—A Missionary Activity," *Ensign,* May, 1975, p. 69.

4. Scott, Richard G. "The Joy of Living the Great Plan of Happiness," *Ensign,* November, 1996, p. 73.

5. McConkie, Bruce R. "Come Know the Lord Jesus," *Ensign,* May 1977, p. 12.

6. Poelman, Ronald E. "Adversity and the Divine Purpose of Mortality," *Ensign,* May 1989, p. 23.

7. Damiani, Adhemar, "The Merciful Plan of the Great Creator," *Ensign,* March 2004, p. 8.

8. Smith, Joseph Fielding. "The Most Important Knowledge," *Ensign,* May 1971, p. 2.

9. "I Am A Child of God," Hymn #301, LDS Hymnal ©The Church of Jesus Christ of Latter-day Saints, chorus used only once at the end.

10. Hinckley, Gordon B. "Come Listen to a Prophet's Voice: You Are a Child of God," *Friend,* May 2003, p. 3.

11. McConkie, Bruce R. The Purifying Power of Gethsemane," *Ensign,* May 1985, p. 9.

12. Eyring, Henry B. "Write Upon My Heart," *Ensign,* November 2000, p. 85.

13. Kimball, Edward L. *Teachings of Spencer W. Kimball,* 1982, p. 204.

14. Faust, James E. "He Healeth the Broken in Heart," *Ensign,* July, 2005, p. 2.

15. Brockbank, Bernard P. "Knowing God," *Ensign*, July 1972, p. 121.

16. Hinckley, Gordon B. "To Single Adults," *Ensign*, June, 1989, p. 72.

17. Hinckley, Gordon B. "Taking the Gospel to Britain: A Declaration of Vision, Faith, Courage, and Truth," *Ensign*, July 1987, page 2.

18. Faust, James E. "He Healeth the Broken in Heart," *Ensign*, July, 2005, p. 2.

19. "I'm Trying To Be Like Jesus," *Children's Songbook of The Church of Jesus Christ of Latter-day Saints*, p. 78.

20. Wirthlin, Joseph B. "The Virtue of Kindness," *Ensign*, May 2005, p. 26.

21. Hinckley, Gordon B. "To Single Adults," *Ensign*, June 1989, p. 72.

22. Maxwell, Neal A. "Remember How Merciful The Lord Hath Been," *Ensign*, May 2004, p. 44.

23. Brockbank, Bernard P. "Knowing God," *Ensign*, July 1972, p. 121.

24. "Love One Another," *Children's Songbook of The Church of Jesus Christ of Latter-day Saints*, p. 136.

25. Hales, Robert D. "Belonging To A Ward Family," *Ensign*, March 1995, p. 15.

26. Edgley, Richard C. "The Empowerment of Humility," *Ensign*, November 2003, p. 97.

27. Hales, Robert D. "Belonging To A Ward Family," *Ensign*, March 1995, p. 15.

28. Faust, James E. "A Vision of What Can Be," *Ensign*, March 1996, p. 10.

29. Carmack, John K. "To My Single Friends," *Ensign*, March 1989, p. 27.

30. Hinckley, Gordon B. "A Conversation With Single Adults," *Ensign*, March 1997, p. 58.

ABOUT THE AUTHOR

Ronald J. Hammond was born in Atlanta, Georgia. He served in the Switzerland Geneva Mission from1982-1984. He met his wife, Alisa, at Ricks College. They have six children, one daughter-in-law, two dogs, and more than twenty years together. Ron has taught Education Week classes at BYU-Idaho and at Utah. He has also taught at regional LDS singles conferences in Utah Valley, St. George, and Ogden. He earned his Ph.D. in Family Studies-Sociology from BYU in 1991. After graduating, Ron taught one year at Case Western Reserve University and is in his 14th year of teaching at Utah Valley State College as a Professor of Sociology.